The Elizabethan
Secret Service

The Elizabethan Secret Service

ALISON PLOWDEN

HARVESTER WHEATSHEAF

ST. MARTIN'S PRESS

First published in England in 1991 by
Harvester Wheatsheaf
66 Wood Lane End, Hemel Hempstead
Hertfordshire HP2 4RG
A division of
Simon & Schuster International Group

First published in the United States of America in 1991
by St. Martin's Press, Inc., 175 Fifth Avenue,
New York, N.Y. 10010
ISBN 0-312-06716-X

Printed and bound in Great Britain by
BPCC Wheatons Ltd, Exeter

British Library Cataloguing in Publication Data

Plowden, Alison
  The Elizabethan secret service.
  1. Secret services, history
  I. Title
  327.1209

  ISBN 0-7108-1152-7

Library of Congress Cataloging-in-Publication Data

Plowden, Alison.
  The Elizabethan secret service / Alison Plowden.
    p.   cm.
  Includes index.
  ISBN 0-312-06716-X
  1. Great Britain—History—Elizabeth, 1558-1603.   2. Great
Britain—Foreign relations—1558-1603.   3. Secret service—England—
History—16th century.   4. Espionage, British—History—16th
century.   I. Title.
DA356.P56   1991
941.05′5—dc20   91-4242
                                                                        CIP

Contents

	A note on sources	vii
CHAPTER ONE	A Florentine gentleman	1
CHAPTER TWO	Certain money in gold to be conveyed into Scotland . . .	25
CHAPTER THREE	The English harvest	49
CHAPTER FOUR	The sacred enterprise	76
CHAPTER FIVE	Sweet England's pride	104
CHAPTER SIX	Gunpowder treason and plot	130
	Index	152

A note on sources

—————◆—————

These notes mention only those works which I have found most helpful in writing this book and are not intended to be more than a general guide.

Indispensable, of course, was *Mr Secretary Walsingham and the Policy of Queen Elizabeth*, in 3 vols. by Conyers Read, Oxford, 1925 (the only scholarly life of Walsingham) also *Mr Secretary Cecil and Queen Elizabeth*, Conyers Read, 1955 and *Lord Burghley and Queen Elizabeth*, Conyers Read, 1960.

There is an enormous amount of material in print, both contemporary and modern, covering every aspect of the controversial career of Mary Queen of Scots, but *The First Trial of Mary Queen of Scots* by Gordon Donaldson, 1969, provides a valuable and scholarly guide to the proceedings at York and Westminster in 1568 which saw the beginning of the Norfolk marriage project leading to the Ridolfi Plot. For a modern, Catholic account of the Norfolk and Ridolfi affairs, see *The Dangerous Queen*, Francis Edwards, 1964, and *The Marvellous Chance*, Francis Edward, 1968; also *Thomas Howard 4th Duke of Norfolk*, Neville Williams, 1964.

For the documents in the case – letters, depositions, confessions interrogations, etc. – see *The Hardwicke State Papers*, 2 vols. 1778, by Philip Yorke, second earl of Hardwicke. *The Burghley State Papers*, vol. 1, ed. Samuel Haynes, 1740 and vol. 2 ed. William Murdin, 1759 and *Illustrations of British History*, E. Lodge, 3 vols., 1838. See also William Camden's *Historie of the most renowned and virtuous Princess Elizabeth, late Queen of England*, 1630. Negotiations with the Queen of Scots and the Scottish government can be followed in Calendar of State Papers, Scottish, ed. J. Bain, vol. 2, Edinburgh 1898 – 1900. For the machinations of Philip of Spain's ambassadors, Guerau de Spes and Bernardino de Mendoza, see Calendar of State Papers, Spanish, Elizabeth, ed. M. A. S. Hume, vols. 2 and 3, 1892–4, and for additional reports from abroad, for example the despatches of Henry Norris and Queen Elizabeth's other ambassadors and agents in various European countries, see Calendar of State Papers, Foreign, Elizabeth, eds. J. Stevenson *et al.* vols. 1 – 8, 1863–71.

The text of the Bull of Excommunications, Regnans in Excelsis, is printed in Camden and also in Father Pollen's *English Catholics in the Reign of Elizabeth*. Bishop Jewel's counter-blast – 'A view of a seditious Bull' – can be found in *The Works of John Jewel*, Parker Society, 1850.

For the general reaction in England to the St. Bartholomew's Day Massacre, see *Annals of the Reformation*, John Strype, Oxford, 1824. The Henry Cockyn affair can be followed in C.S.P. Scotland, vol. 10 and the antics of Don John of Austria and Thomas Stukeley are reported in the C.S.P. Spanish and Foreign, Elizabeth.

A great deal has been written about the English mission and the predicament of the Catholic minority in 16th century England – most of it from the Catholic point of view – but some useful general surveys are *England and the Catholic Church Under Queen Elizabeth* A. O. Meyer, trans. J. R. McKee, 1916, re-issued 1967; *Papists and Puritans*, P. McGrath, 1967 and *The English Catholics in the Reign of Elizabeth*, J. M. Pollen, 1920. Much contemporary material concerning the missionary priests and their activities has been printed by the Catholic Record Society, see for example the *Letters and Memorials of Father Robert Parsons*, ed. L. Hicks, C. R. S. No. 39 (1942). For an account of Edmund Campion's capture at Lyford, see *Edmund Campion* by Richard Simpson, 1867, which prints a number of letters and documents. Lord Burghley's *Execution of Justice*, representing the official view of Queen Elizabeth's government, is printed in Somers Tracts, vol. 1, ed. Walter Scott, 1809, in the *Harleian Miscellany* and *Holinshed's Chronicle*.

The Lennox–Guise–Throckmorton affair can be followed in the C. S. P. Scottish, ed. W. K. Boyd, vol. 6 and C. S. P. Spanish, Elizabeth, vol. 3 See also the C. S. P. Foreign, Elizabeth; the *Letters of Robert Parsons* and the *Letters and Memorials of William Allen*, ed. T. F. Knox, 1882. The official account of the Throckmorton Plot is printed in vol. 3 of the *Harleian Miscellany* and that of the Parry Plot in *Holinshed's Chronicle*, 2nd ed., J. Hooker, vol. 3, 1587. See also *An Elizabethan Problem* by L. Hicks, 1964, which examines the dubious career of Thomas Morgan. There is a comprehensive account of the Babington affair in *Mary Queen of Scots and the Babington Plot*, J. H. Pollen, Scot. Hist. Soc. 3rd series, III, 1922 and *The Letter Books of Sir Amias Paulet*, John Morris, 1874 describes the measures taken to isolate Mary.

Many of the letters of Walsingham's agent, Thomas Rogers, alias Nicholas Berden, are printed with the correspondence of Philip Howard, Earl of Arundel, Catholic Record Society, no. 21. For two contrasting views on *The Fame of Sir Edward Stafford*, see Conyers Read in the *American Historical Review*, 1915, and J.E. Neale in the *English Historical Review*, 1929.

For the post–Walsingham period there is an interesting study of the Bacon brothers in *Golden Lads* by Daphne du Maurier, 1975 and several biographies of the Earl of Essex, for example, G. B. Harrison's *The Life and Death of Robert Devereux, Earl of Essex* 1937, and *Robert, Earl of Essex: An Elizabethan Icarus*, Robert Lacey, 1971. See also *Lives and Letters of the Devereux, Earls of Essex*, W. B. Devereux, 1853; Thomas Birch, *Memoirs of the Reign of Queen Elizabeth*, 2 vols., 1754 for the correspondence of Anthony Bacon; and *Treason and Plot*, M. A. S. Hume, 1901. For the affair of Dr. Lopez see Birch and Hume, but also C.S.P. Spanish, Elizabeth, vol. 4 and 'The Conspiracy of Dr. Lopez' Arthur Dimock, *English Historical Review*, July 1894. Robert Cecil has attracted few biographers but see *A Life of Robert Cecil, 1st Earl of Salisbury*, A. Cecil, 1915. Cecil's correspondence with James is printed in *Correspondence of King James VI of Scotland with Sir Robert Cecil and others* ed. John Bruce, Camden Society 1861 (this also contains an appendix which prints material on the clandestine dealings of James, Essex, Mountjoy *et al.* in 1600-1601).

There is a voluminous literature devoted to the great gunpowder treason of which the following is a brief selection: *The Gunpowder Plot*, H. R. Williamson, 1951; *Guy Fawkes: the real story of the Gunpowder Plot*, Francis Edwardes S. J., 1969, *The Condition of the Catholics under James I: Father Gerard's Narrative of the Gunpowder Plot*, ed. John Morris, 1871; *A Narrative of the Gun Powder Plot*, David Jardine, 1857; and *Gunpowder Treason and Plot*, C. Northcote Parkinson, 1976.

CHAPTER ONE

A Florentine gentleman

There are three ordinary spies in England, all Spaniards: one John Delgado, who lies in the ambassador's house; Peter Benavides, who resorts thither; and Diego Ridiera, a tall man of person, eyed like a cat, whose charge is to go about England . . . . Also there is a man who has but one eye and a cut over the face, the one part thereof burnt with gunpowder, who is sent to work treason to her Highness.

Thus Henry Norris, Queen Elizabeth's envoy in France, reporting from Paris in the spring of 1570.

In the sixteenth century, as in the twentieth, espionage and diplomacy more often than not went hand in hand. At a time when western European diplomacy was almost exclusively preoccupied with the deadly power game of Catholic versus Protestant, and the ideological battle lines were being drawn, a supply of reliably accurate secret intelligence was recognized as an essential weapon by both sides – but especially by the emergent Protestant states headed by England, the most aggressively successful Protestant state of them all.

The success story of Protestant England represented a source of profound and ongoing irritation to many of her continental neighbours, for this small, seemingly insignificant off-shore island – only half an island, in fact – which twice in a generation had chosen defiantly to cut itself off from the community of Catholic Christendom, was yet able to exert a most potent influence over the calculations of the two great Catholic power blocs of France and Spain. It is only necessary to look at the map to see why. England's

1

command of the vital shipping lanes of the Channel and the Narrow Seas lent her a strategic importance which bore no relation to her size, plus, it was felt in some circles, a quite unfair advantage in the field of international politics.

The King of Spain, with an empire stretching from the Mediterranean to the Low Countries and across the Atlantic to the territories of New Spain, was especially vulnerable to any threat to his seaborne communications, and had been given an unnerving demonstration of what this could mean in practice when, in the late autumn of 1568, half a dozen small vessels *en route* for Antwerp were driven by bad weather and French pirates to seek shelter in the English south coast ports of Plymouth and Southampton. These ships were laden with gold coin intended for the army currently engaged in putting down a rebellion in the Spanish Netherlands and they offered the Queen of England, chronically short of ready cash, a temptation which was hardly to be resisted. Elizabeth did not resist – not once she discovered that the gold could still technically be regarded as the property of the Genoese banking houses which were lending it to King Philip – and on 28 December she blandly informed the Spanish ambassador that, having been assured that the money did not yet belong to the King, she had decided to borrow it herself.

The Italians had no objection to transferring their business to another client, but the hijacking of the payships did nothing to sweeten Anglo-Spanish relations, already less than cordial, and the repercussions of the affair rumbled bad-temperedly on for several months. Nevertheless, in the winter of 1568/9 those in a position to know were of the opinion that the most immediate threat to the Queen's security came from France.

The previous May the English government had been considerably taken aback by the precipitate arrival on the coast of Cumbria of that well-known *femme fatale*, Mary Queen of Scots, deposed and imprisoned by her ungrateful subjects and now fleeing for her life with nothing in the world but the clothes she stood up in. Mary had claimed political asylum, together with military and/or financial aid against her rebels, from Elizabeth, her tender cousin and sister queen – an apparently straightforward request which, however, positively bristled with political man-traps.

It was not just that Mary was a Catholic, or that she was widely believed to have arranged the death of her second husband prior to marrying his murderer, which worried the Council in London. Nor was it just that, as Elizabeth's senior cousin, she had been tactless enough to press for parliamentary recognition of her title as heiress to the English throne. The real impediment to reaching an understanding with the Queen of Scots was, as it had always been, the fact that she had 'heretofore openly challenged the crown of England, not as a second person after the Queen's majesty, but afore her.' This went back ten years, to the time when, as the teenage bride of the Dauphin, Mary had been proclaimed Queen of England by Henri II of France. True, she had then been little more than a child and subject to the authority of husband and father-in-law, but even after her return to Scotland in the early 1560s, a widow and her own mistress, she had still contrived to find one plausible excuse after another for not ratifying the Treaty of Edinburgh, in which the French had rather grudgingly conceded that the realms of England and Ireland did indeed belong by right to 'the serene lady and princess Elizabeth'.

Mary, always 'the very pith and marrow of sweet eloquence', had worked hard to persuade Elizabeth to give her the *de jure* recognition she craved, assuring her dearest cousin at every opportunity of the purity of her intentions, the absolute sincerity of her friendship and esteem – assurances which Elizabeth received with private scepticism and public refusals to settle the succession on the Queen of Scots 'by order of Parliament'. In off-the-record conversation with the Scottish envoy, William Maitland, she was quite prepared to admit that she regarded Mary as her nearest kinswoman and her natural and lawful heir, but she would not make it official. When Maitland urged that surely this would be the best way to cement the alliance between them, Elizabeth did not agree. 'Think you that I could love my own winding sheet?' she had enquired with brutal frankness. And there were other considerations. 'I know the inconstancy of the people of England', remarked their Queen, 'how they ever mislike the present government and have their eyes fixed upon the person that is next to succeed, and naturally men be so disposed.'

The problem of who should be next to succeed their childless Queen (especially after Elizabeth had nearly died of smallpox in the autumn of 1562) was to go on exercising the minds of all politically conscious Englishmen throughout the reign, but Elizabeth herself remained convinced that if once 'it were certainly known in the world who should succeed her, she would never think herself in sufficient surety.' From her own past experience as a 'second person', she knew, none better, that the heir to the throne inevitably became a magnet for all shades of social and political disaffection, and while the Queen of England believed her subjects to be generally loyal, 'yet is nowhere so great perfection that all are content'. She was careful not to mention the extra factor which made Mary so especially dangerous as a rival – that in the eyes of orthodox Roman Catholics everywhere the Queen of Scots possessed an undoubted legal and moral right to challenge her English cousin's crown, not indeed as a second person, but 'afore her'. Orthodox Roman Catholics, of whom, to the regret of the ruling Protestant party, a sizeable minority still survived in England, had after all every excuse for preferring the claims of King Henry VIII's great-niece, born in undisputedly lawful wedlock, to those of his younger daughter, born during the lifetime of his first wife and of a marriage which he himself had later so violently repudiated.

The problem of what to do about Mary had been the subject of much anxious deliberation by the English Privy Council in the weeks following her arrival. The Spanish ambassador thought that on the whole 'these people' were not sorry to have the Queen of Scots in their hands, but, he went on, 'if they keep her as in prison, it will probably scandalise all neighbouring princes, and if she remain free and able to communicate with her friends, great suspicions will be aroused.' The contemporary historian William Camden could also see the obvious drawbacks attached to detaining Mary against her will. She would be only too likely to

> draw many daily to her part which favoured her title to the crown of England, who would kindle the coals of her ambition, and leave nothing unassayed whereby they might set the crown upon her head. Foreign ambassadors would further her counsels and designs; and the Scots then would not fail her, when they should see so rich a booty offered them.

Unfortunately, however, no other practicable course of action suggested itself in the short term. Any chance of finding a formula by which Mary Stewart could safely be restored to her northern kingdom was at best remote, and would depend on the successful outcome of delicate, time-consuming negotiations with the current regime in Edinburgh – negotiations in which possession of the

Queen of Scots' person would be an essential bargaining counter. For this reason, if no other (and there were a number of others), there was no question of allowing Mary to return to France, the country where she had been educated, had reigned briefly as Queen Consort and where she still had powerful family connections, headed by her uncle the Cardinal of Lorraine and her cousin Henry, Duke of Guise, both of whom could be relied upon to stir up a hornet's nest of intrigue on her behalf.

English Protestants had long regarded the ultra-Catholic, politically ambitious Guise clan with the deepest suspicion, and by midsummer 1568 Henry Norris was relaying warnings of dastardly Guisard plots, and of their plans to rescue the captive Queen of Scotland. In July he was asking most earnestly that Elizabeth should pay special attention to her safety, 'for there are certain Italians sent into England by the Cardinal of Lorraine to practise against her.' The Cardinal, he reminded William Cecil, 'being a most cruel enemy to the Queen and her country, will leave nothing unattempted that may be to her prejudice.' In October, Norris received a visit at nine o'clock one night from an anonymous informant 'sent from one of honour to advertise that about the end of this month an enterprise should be attempted against the Queen as also against the Earl of Moray (now ruling Scotland in the name of Mary's two-year-old son) by the Cardinal of Lorraine.' Another rumour flying around Paris about a plot to release the Queen of Scots implicated an English nobleman, but the ambassador had not been able to discover his identity. Hard information, in fact, remained disturbingly hard to come by and in August Norris had advised Mr Secretary Cecil to employ one Captain François to pursue enquiries further. Captain François, otherwise Franchot or Franchiotto the Italian, was an experienced undercover agent who had been for many years in the service of the French crown, but was now apparently resident in London.

William Cecil was a busy man and delegated the task of contacting Captain François to his friend and protégé Francis Walsingham, who had spent some time abroad and spoke French and Italian fluently. A committed Protestant, zealous for the cause of religion, Walsingham wasted no time in seeking out Franchiotto the Italian. But although that individual was free with warnings of plots, advising Queen Elizabeth to take extra precautions against poison and hinting darkly at a conspiracy being hatched jointly by

France and Spain 'for the alteration of religion and the advancement of the Queen of Scots to the crown', his intelligence was disappointingly short on detail – so much so, indeed, that Walsingham sometimes wondered if it was worth passing on. He always did, though. Walsingham always believed in being safe rather than sorry.

Actually, if intelligence coming in from abroad continued to be on the level of gossip, rumour and wishful thinking, it was for the good enough reason that in 1568/9 there were no plans worth mentioning to subvert the Protestant regime in England and advance the Queen of Scots – the Catholic powers were too busy with their own problems. In France religious civil war still raged intermittently and Spain was preoccupied with suppressing the revolt in the Netherlands. Nevertheless, William Cecil and a growing number of other sober God-fearing Englishmen viewed the international situation with the gravest foreboding, dreading 'a conspiracy of the Pope, King Philip, the French king and sundry potentates of Italy to employ all their forces for the subversion of the professors of the gospel.' It was always Cecil's nightmare that sooner or later the Catholic powers would combine against Protestant England. The fact that they had not already done so was, in his opinion, to be attributed to good luck or God's providence, and Cecil did not believe in trusting entirely to God's providence. The French Huguenots did occasionally win a battle or a grudging measure of toleration, but their destruction looked like being only a matter of time. Nor was it probable that the defiant Calvinists of Holland and Zealand could long survive the calculated campaign of terror being waged by the Duke of Alva and his notorious army of Blackbeards, while already the pressure on Philip's other flank by the Turks in the Mediterranean was easing. As soon as France and Spain were free of their internal problems, they would surely turn their attention jointly across the English Channel, where Mary Stewart was waiting for them. The English Secretary of State was never one for looking on the bright side, but he was unquestionably a highly practised and intelligent observer of the European scene and he placed no reliance whatever on the chances of peaceful co-existence between the rival ideologies. By the close of the 1560s he saw a final confrontation of Catholic and Protestant, of might against right, as inevitable and not long to be delayed.

As it happened, the troubles which afflicted Protestant England in 1569 came from within rather than without, although they were

predictably centred upon the Queen of Scots. After due consideration and some intensive behind-the-scenes horse-trading, the
Queen of England had announced her intention of holding a public
enquiry into the dispute between the Scottish nobility and their
Queen. The lords who had had the effrontery to depose and
imprison her were to be summoned to appear before a panel of
English commissioners and required to justify their actions. Mary
herself would be represented and given every opportunity to put
her side of the case – indeed the enquiry was being officially
portrayed as an investigation into the Queen of Scotland's com-
plaint against her rebellious subjects. After hearing the evidence,
Elizabeth proposed to act as adjudicator and would either restore
Mary to her throne or, failing that, make every effort to persuade
the parties to accept an honourable compromise.

The enquiry, or conference, opened in York on 10 October 1568
and was to see the first appearance of the much-discussed Casket
Letters, which, if genuine, seemed to offer proof positive of Mary's
guilty knowledge of the murder at Kirk o'Field. It also saw the
opening moves in a long and complicated sequence of events later to
become known as the Ridolfi plot. The commissioners nominated
by Elizabeth to meet the Scots were headed by Thomas Howard,
fourth Duke of Norfolk, England's premier nobleman and only
duke, whose rank may have given the status necessary for presiding
over such an assembly but who, unfortunately, did not possess the
equally necessary mental dexterity and specialist knowledge. Certainly, Sir Ralph Sadler, the veteran Scottish expert, did not think
he was up to the job and the Duke himself approached it with
misgiving. 'This cause', he told William Cecil, 'is the doubtfullest
and dangerest that ever I dealt in', and went on to complain that
while 'there be some few in this company that mean plainly and
truly, so there be others that seek wholly to serve their own private
turns.' He did not add that he, too, had some private turns to serve,
for it was at York that he was first propositioned by Maitland of
Lethington, who suggested that he might care to consider putting
himself forward as a suitor for the Queen of Scots' hand in
marriage. Norfolk had just been given a sight of copies of the still
highly classified Casket Letters and had expressed suitably shocked
horror over the depth of moral turpitude they revealed, but
murderess and adulteress or not, Mary Stewart remained a matri-
monial prize second only to Elizabeth Tudor, and Norfolk, a

widower in his early thirties, was sufficiently tempted to 'give good ear' to Maitland's persuasive sales talk.

The idea of solving the problem of Mary by means of an arranged marriage with some trustworthy and sufficiently high-ranking Englishman was not a new one – Elizabeth herself had explored its possibilities back in the early 1560s, when she had gone so far as to propose her own favourite, Robert Dudley, Earl of Leicester, as a bridegroom for her good sister and cousin. It was, however, an ultra-sensitive area politically and as reports of a potential under-standing between her presumptive heiress and her mightiest subject began to reach London, an immediate change was noticed in Elizabeth's attitude. 'The Queen's Majesty', wrote William Cecil, 'is now at a pinch so careful for her own surety and state as I perceive the Queen of Scots shall not be advanced to greater credit than her cause will serve. And I think that is rather to put her back than to further her.' It certainly looked that way when, at a Council meeting on 30 October, it was agreed that the Earl of Moray should be encouraged to produce the Casket Letters in open court and press the murder charge against Mary. Four days later Elizabeth announced that the enquiry was to be transferred to Westminster – a change of venue which undoubtedly had a good deal to do with the doubts being cast on Norfolk's good faith.

Thomas Howard occupied a very special place in the Elizabethan hierarchy. As the country's leading aristocrat, with the blood of the old royal house in his veins, and closely related to the Queen through her mother, he commanded immense personal influence and respect in government circles. As a great territorial magnate he commanded personal power on an almost medieval scale. He was also a popular figure, widely regarded as standing aloof from the self-seeking scramble of ordinary career politicians. But now it seemed that even Norfolk had his price and that that price was the Queen of Scotland – a discovery which did more to harden Elizabeth's heart against Mary than all Cecil's well-argued memor-anda. After his return to London in November, Elizabeth asked him outright about the rumours linking his name with the Queen of Scots, and Norfolk denied them. 'No reason', he declared virtuously, 'could move him to like of her that hath been a competitor to the Crown' and in any case he would never marry 'where he could not be sure of his pillow' – an allusion, presumably, to the gory fate of Henry Darnley. Elizabeth did not believe him, but she said nothing and the Duke thought he had satisfied her 'well enough' while resuming discussions with the Scottish Regent Moray (who was also Mary's bastard half-brother), with William Maitland and John Leslie, Bishop of Ross, Mary's principal spokesman and 'ambassador', regarding the marriage project.

In the meantime the enquiry which was to decide the Queen of Scots' future had re-opened in the Painted Chamber at Westminster. Moray duly laid his Eik, or addition to the Scots lords' original statement, before the assembled commissioners, and formally accused Mary of complicity in the murder of Darnley. Mary, for her part, vehemently maintained her innocence, declaring the infamous Casket Letters to be forgeries. She would not, however, deign to answer the charges against her except as one Queen to another in a private interview with Elizabeth, which Elizabeth refused to grant until Mary had been 'in some wise purged' of guilt. The resultant impasse was finally resolved on 10 January 1569 when, in a statement issued by the Secretary of State, it was announced that, since nothing had been deduced against Moray and his party 'that may impair their honour and allegiance', the Queen's Majesty of England had agreed to allow them 'at their pleasure to depart'. Equally, it appeared that nothing had been 'sufficiently produced nor shown by them against the Queen their sovereign whereby the Queen of England should conceive or take any evil opinion against the Queen her good sister'; but Mary was not going anywhere. The Queen of Scots had fled to the Queen of England for protection, and protection she was going to get. How could Elizabeth hope to order a just and permanent redress of her cousin's grievances until Mary had replied to the very serious charges which had been made against her? The Queen of England had made a solemn and public promise to solve the Queen of Scotland's problems, and until that promise had been satisfactorily fulfilled, she could not in honour or safety let her leave the country. And there, for the time being, the matter rested, with Moray back in Scotland and Mary transferred to the custody of the Earl and Countess of Shrewsbury, who were instructed to accommodate her in one or other of their numerous mansions in the north Midlands and treat her with all the respect due to her royal rank.

As an interim settlement, it had a good deal to recommend it from the English point of view. The position of the friendly, reliably Protestant regime in Edinburgh had been strengthened and a thin cloak of justification thrown over Mary's continued detention, for although the Casket Letters remained officially confidential, their contents were by this time sufficiently widely known to have scandalised an influential section of English public opinion. On the debit side, of course, Elizabeth was left with the expense, the anxiety and social embarrassment attached to keeping the Queen of Scots to all intents and purposes a state prisoner – a situation which the Queen of Scots had no intention of accepting without a struggle. She had, in fact, already embarked on her long, tortuous and ultimately disastrous career of intrigue, using all the weapons at her disposal. 'The Queen of Scotland', wrote the newly arrived Spanish ambassador early in October 1568, 'knows how to ingratiate herself with her keepers, and has many on her side.'

Mary was then still at Bolton Castle in Yorkshire, an area where Catholicism was strong, and Don Guerau de Spes thought it should not be difficult to release her and 'even raise a great revolt against this Queen [Elizabeth]'. But it would obviously be better if the King of Spain did not appear to be concerned in such an affair and de Spes would do nothing unless instructed. Meanwhile, he set about organizing his own network of informants, making contact with Mary's friends and opening a direct channel of communication with the captive herself. 'I have', he told Philip at the end of October, '. . . obtained a new cipher with the Queen of Scotland, the old one having been lost.' Soon couriers were going regularly to and fro with letters and messages, and early in the new year Don Guerau was able to report triumphantly: 'The Queen of Scotland told my servant to convey to me the following words – "Tell the ambassador that, if his master will help me, I shall be Queen of England in three months, and mass shall be said all over the country." '

In fact, de Spes' instructions had been conciliatory. He was to salute Elizabeth 'gaily and graciously'; serve and gratify her on every possible occasion and do his best to keep her on good terms, assuring her that the King of Spain would always return her friendship as her good neighbour and brother. In the summer of 1568, with the Netherlands in open rebellion, the last thing Philip needed was to become embroiled in any unpleasantness with England. After the episode of the pay-ships he was irritated enough to agree that there was much to be said for the notion of deposing the Queen of England and giving her crown to the Queen of Scots; but, desirable though this would be for the restoration of religion, the King does not seem to have regarded it as being a very serious possibility, merely referring the matter to the Duke of Alva for his consideration with a request to be kept informed.

Philip was not alone in his exasperation over the seizure of the pay-ships. An important group of English councillors, nominally led by the Duke of Norfolk, looked on it as an unwise and unnecessary provocation and an alarming instance of the growing power of William Cecil. This faction, which included the Earls of Arundel and Pembroke, the Marquis of Northampton and possibly also the old Marquis of Winchester, favoured a policy of conciliation towards Spain and the cutting off of aid to the French Huguenot rebels. They wanted the release of the Queen of Scots from detention, her recognition as heiress presumptive and her marriage to the Duke of Norfolk. They also wanted to get rid of the upstart Mr Secretary Cecil, in which they could count on the support of the Earl of Leicester. Towards the end of February 1569 Norfolk and Arundel sent Roberto Ridolfi, 'a great friend of theirs and mine', to tell Guerau de Spes about their hopes of being able to overthrow 'the present accursed government and raise another Catholic one, bringing the Queen to consent thereto.'

The intention appears to have been to ambush Cecil at the Council table with some trumped-up charge of mismanaging the nation's affairs and hustle him straight off to the Tower, where, experience suggested, 'means to undo him would not be far to seek.' A similar ploy, masterminded by Norfolk's grandfather, had succeeded effortlessly against Secretary of State Thomas Cromwell in King Henry VIII's time. It failed on this occasion because Cecil was too wary and too well informed to be taken unawares, because the present Duke of Norfolk was not the man his grandfather had been and because, above all, Queen Elizabeth was not the kind of monarch her father had been. She might drive her loyal servants to the brink of nervous breakdown by some of her little ways, but she was not in the habit of throwing them to the wolves. Forewarned by Cecil, she intervened angrily and decisively on his behalf, forcing the conspirators into ignominious retreat. Their unofficial plans for settling the Queen of Scots' future, however, remained very much in being.

The Norfolk marriage project attracted support not only from Catholics dissatisfied with the present government, from conservative peers – especially impoverished feudal magnates like the Earls

11

of Northumberland and Westmorland, to whom it seemed to offer renewed hope for the future – but also from those at the other end of the religious spectrum, from men like Nicholas Throckmorton and even the Regent Moray himself, who were afraid that Elizabeth meant to restore Mary without adequate safeguards and who thought that 'by this marriage her highness and the realm might take commodity.' The fact that Mary was at this time still married to the unfortunate Earl of Bothwell, now languishing in a Danish gaol, entered no one's calculations, except as a trifling impediment easily dispensed with.

Mary had no personal knowledge of Norfolk – they never did meet – and when the proposal was first put to her, her reaction was one of caution. The important thing, she said, was to regain her freedom of action. It would be time enough to talk about marriage after that. But as it began to be borne in on her that marriage to Norfolk offered her her best, possibly her only, immediate hope of freedom, her enthusiasm increased and, in response to an approach made at the beginning of June 1569, she agreed to consider the Duke's suit, although stipulating that Elizabeth's consent must be sought. In fact, she was eager for the match and had already begun to correspond affectionately with Norfolk. By the end of June the French ambassador in London reported that the affair seemed so far advanced that he thought it could not fail to proceed. 'The Queen of Scots', he wrote, 'appears not only to consent but very strongly to desire it', and a month later Guerau de Spes believed it was all but settled.

Mary's and Norfolk's apologists have always insisted that there was nothing treasonable or even disloyal about the marriage scheme by itself. Mary's release was to be conditional on her marriage to an Englishman (Norfolk) who would be the guarantor of her good behaviour, and the marriage itself conditional on her undertaking to relinquish all claims prejudicial to Queen Elizabeth, to abandon any alliance with France in favour of 'a league made betwixt England and Scotland', and to see that in future the government of Scotland was always to 'the contentation of the Queen of England'. In spite of this, it was noticeable that none of the scheme's promoters, least of all the bridegroom elect, could quite bring themselves to mention it to the Queen of England. In the end it was the Earl of Leicester who decided the time had come to spill the beans and the Queen then had it out with Norfolk, commanding him on his allegiance to deal no more in the Scottish matter. Elizabeth was under no illusions as to who would be the dominant partner in such an alliance, or what the consequences would be for herself. She told the Earl of Leicester grimly that if it took place she would be in the Tower inside four months.

One way and another it was an uneasy summer. At the beginning of August, de Spes reported that the Duke of Norfolk and his friends were very busy trying to get Mary declared the Queen's successor and added hopefully that 'there certainly will be some turmoil about it.' Six weeks later the ambassador still thought the marriage would go ahead in spite of Elizabeth's prohibition: 'I do not believe the Duke will desist from his enterprise in consequence. A stronger guard has been placed around the Queen of Scotland', he went on, 'although I have understood that she will, nevertheless, soon find herself at liberty. . . . All the north is ready, and only awaits the release of the Queen of Scotland.'

Rumblings of serious disenchantment with central government had been audible from north of the Trent for some time and when, at the end of September, the Duke of Norfolk suddenly bolted for his East Anglian estates, where, he was wont to boast, he thought himself as good a prince as any, the Queen not unnaturally took alarm. The whole court, according to William Camden, 'hung in suspense and fear lest he should break forth into rebellion.' 'I do not know what will happen', de Spes told King Philip on 30 September; 'but I understand, considering the number of the Duke's friends in England, he cannot be ruined, except by pusillanimity, and the Queen of Scotland has sent to urge him to behave valiantly and not to fear for his life which God would protect.' But the shifty Norfolk, who was by this time deeply involved not only with Mary but the insurrectionary plans of the Catholic Earls of Northumberland and Westmorland, had lost his nerve. Elizabeth ordered him back to Court. He sent excuses, pleading an ague. The Queen told him to come anyway, by litter if necessary, and by the second week of October he had surrendered to her officers and been consigned to the Tower in preventive detention, William Cecil having advised Her Majesty that, after studying the words of the statute, he could not see how the Duke's actions were 'within the compass of treason'.

Norfolk's principal associates, the Earls of Arundel and Pembroke, Nicholas Throckmorton and his brother-in-law Lord

13

Lumley, were all being required to give an account of themselves, and the government had also begun to take an active interest in the affairs of Roberto Ridolfi, whose name had been appearing at frequent intervals in Guerau de Spes' dispatches during the summer. On 7 October, some four days before the Duke of Norfolk, travelling in the royal barge, was ceremonially conducted by water to the Tower, William Cecil and the Earl of Leicester had written jointly to Francis Walsingham, informing him that 'the Queen's majesty hath commanded us to write to the Lord Mayor of London for the apprehension of Robert Ridolfi, whom her Majesty would have remain in your house without conference until he may be examined of certain matters which touch her Majesty very nearly.'

Ridolfi, usually referred to as 'a merchant' or 'a wealthy merchant', was a Florentine, member of a cadet branch of one of the city's noblest families, who, with his parents, owned a controlling interest in one of Florence's most important merchant banks. Together with men like Benedict Spinola, Thomas Fiesco and Guido Cavalcanti, Roberto Ridolfi belonged to a banking fraternity based in the cities of Florence, Genoa and Milan which exercised an incalculable influence over the course of European politics. It might have been expected that such a consortium would have favoured the Catholic cause, but the Italians were first and foremost businessmen with whom the creditworthiness of their customers counted for a good deal more than their religious convictions. Not that they were averse to the Catholic cause, if the price was right; and it seems that Roberto Ridolfi had, from 1566 onwards, been acting as an unofficial papal nuncio, entrusted by Pius V with considerable sums of money for distribution among the English Catholics and instructions to encourage the formation of a league of Catholic sympathizers among the English nobility.

Ridolfi was particularly well placed to undertake such a commission. His family had long-standing business connections in England and he himself had been living and working in London at least since the beginning of the 1560s – some accounts say earlier still. During this period he had built up an impressive list of contacts in high places and, it would appear, a useful reputation as an honest broker. In December 1568 the great City of London financier Thomas Gresham was calling on him to arrange letters of credit on Germany for 12,000 ducats for one of the Queen's special envoys, and the following June William Cecil invited him to dinner to discuss the negotiations aimed at lifting the various trading sanctions imposed after the unfortunate affair of the Spanish pay-ships. This at the same time that Ridolfi was carrying messages to Guerau de Spes from Norfolk and his cronies outlining their plans for encompassing Cecil's downfall and promising that they would ensure the repayment in full of the bullion seized on the Secretary's orders!

Bold, talkative, plausible and naturally meddlesome, Ridolfi was the archetypal Mr Fix-it, trotting between Court and counting house, embassy and ducal residence with messages, money bags, schemes and suggestions, while collecting his 10 per cent impartially from the Vatican, from France and Spain, from the Queen of England's treasury and the high-class customers of his bank. It was the size of the bills of exchange which had recently begun to reach him from Flanders, plus the discovery that these 'great sums of money' were finding their way into the hands of Mary Queen of Scots' factotum, the Bishop of Ross, which had alerted William Cecil, and again he turned to Francis Walsingham, as one whose loyalty and discretion were absolute, to undertake the task of investigating the busy Italian.

Under interrogation, Ridolfi admitted to having been instrumental in conveying funds from abroad on behalf of the Queen of Scots and to making loans to the Bishop of Ross and the Duke of Norfolk, but only in the normal course of his business. He also admitted having been 'made privy to the matter of marriage betwixt the Queen of Scots and the duke', and went on to hint that there were certain other matters on which he would not declare his knowledge 'but only to the Queen's Majesty'. This was duly reported by Walsingham and on 19 October another letter arrived over the joint signatures of Cecil and Leicester commending his diligence and instructing him to tell Ridolfi to put all his private information in writing 'and so sealed up to be sent unto her Majesty'. At the same time, a further list of questions was enclosed, to which truthful answers were to be extracted from the prisoner.

Four days later Cecil wrote again. The Queen, having received Ridolfi's letter 'with her own proper hand', had accepted it in good part – as far as it went. But she was still by no means satisfied that he had told all he knew, and if he really wanted her favour as much as he said he did, he would have to 'more amply explicate' – especially any 'conferences and practices to him well known concerning the Queen of Scots'. But the general tone of the letter was conciliatory, almost apologetic. It was to be explained that, while it was customary for a suspect's papers to be examined for possibly incriminating evidence, the Queen was anxious that nothing should be done to prejudice Ridolfi's legitimate 'trade of merchandise'. Therefore none of his business rivals would be allowed access to his house and the search of his 'writings and letters' was to be carried out with his permission and in his presence by Francis Walsingham in person, giving every consideration to the preservation of his professional secrets. This was certainly kid-glove treatment and shortly afterwards, in response to another letter from Ridolfi to the Queen, permission was granted for him to receive visitors, send and receive messages and attend to his more urgent business affairs under the supervision of his host.

On 11 November, just over a month from the date of his arrest, Ridolfi was released on his own recognizance of £1,000 and on condition that in future he kept out of politics and any other matters 'not appertaining to himself and the trades of merchandise'. He was to be told that Her Majesty considered he had abused his privileges by meddling in affairs of state and if she had chosen to be severe she could have forced him to confess more than he had. Yet 'having naturally a proper inclination to favour all gentlemen of his country', and hoping that he would keep his promise 'according to his own writing' to stay out of trouble in future, she was graciously pleased to restore his liberty. The following January his £1,000 bond was discharged and no further restrictions placed on his freedom of movement.

It had been a curious little episode and at least one highly respected historian has expressed surprise that Ridolfi got off so easily. William Cecil, in his short and noticeably uninformative account written for publication but seemingly never actually published, simply says that 'upon his [Ridolfi's] submission and offer in writing . . . that he would no more meddle with the Scottish Queen's cause, nor the Duke's, but would live as a merchant according to his profession, he was set at liberty.' Three years later, when he was trying to impress Pope, Gregory XIII, with the importance of his services to English Catholicism, Ridolfi himself boasted that he had been examined on matters sufficiently serious to have secured his beheading twenty-five times over, but thanks to God and his friends, of whom he had many in the Queen's Council, 'all passed off smoothly.'

In view of Francis Walsingham's later reputation, the fact that Ridolfi had been able to outsmart him with such apparent ease is regarded with considerable suspicion in some circles, and one Catholic historian has made out a detailed case to show that Ridolfi was 'turned' during the weeks he spent under Walsingham's roof. On the other hand, it needs to be remembered that in 1569 Walsingham was still relatively inexperienced as a 'searcher of secrets' and may have been genuinely deceived – in a letter to Cecil written the following October, he was describing Ridolfi as one 'who standeth on terms of honesty and reputation' and recommending his employment in the continuing negotiations with Alva in Flanders. Rather than antagonize important Italian banking interests, the Queen's Council may have decided to give Ridolfi the benefit of the doubt. They may have been hoping that, given enough rope he would hang himself – and others. But it is also perfectly possible that he and his interrogators had found themselves able to arrive at a mutually advantageous arrangement. Whatever the truth of the matter, it is not disputed that immediately upon his release he resumed his extra-mural activities as undercover agent for the Vatican and friendly neighbourhood moneylender and confidant to any and all disaffected members of the English peerage.

Ridolfi played no direct part in the abortive rebellion of those outstandingly disaffected members of the peerage, the Earls of Northumberland and Westmorland. The so-called Northern Rising had broken out while he was still in custody and incommunicado but in the months following its collapse he continued to receive commissions from an ill-informed and optimistic papacy authorizing him to pay out large sums of money – up to a hundred thousand crowns – to the English Catholic rebels if they behaved properly, and he had a good deal to do with the publication in May 1570 of the papal bull excommunicating Elizabeth, 'the Servant of Wickedness'.

The promulgation of *Regnans in Excelsis*, which declared 'the pretended Queen of England' to be cut off from the unity of the body of Christ and deprived of her title to her kingdom 'and of all Dominion, Dignity and Privilege whatsoever', not surprisingly provoked a violent popular reaction. Patriotic ballads, broadsheets and pamphlets flooded the market, with much opportunity for merry sport being afforded by the convenient double meaning of the word 'bull'. The Bishop of Salisbury, put up by the Church of

England to answer the papal challenge, found it to be 'a matter of great blasphemy against God and a practice to work much unquietness, sedition and treason'. For, he went on,

> it deposeth the Queen's majesty from her royal seat and teareth the crown from her head; it dischargeth all us her natural subjects from all due obedience; it armeth one side of us against another; it emboldeneth us to burn, to spoil, to rob, to kill, and to cut one another's throat.

How dared the Pope, that 'wilful and unlearned friar', how dared he say that Elizabeth, the right inheritor of the houses of York and Lancaster, accepted by the nobility and joyfully acknowledged by all the commons of the realm, was no lawful Queen? Had Christ ever set himself up against the temporal ruler? demanded Bishop Jewel. Had not Peter said, 'It is the will of God that you obey your prince'? If the English people continued to obey their prince as God had commanded, they would be accursed by the Pope; but if they disobeyed, 'as the Pope requireth', then they would, thundered the Bishop of Salisbury in his peroration, certainly be condemned by the judgement of God.

In fact, condemnation of *Regnans in Excelsis* was pretty well universal. The Holy Father had apparently acted without consulting any of the temporal Catholic princes who, in theory at least, would have the duty of carrying out the deposition of the 'pretended Queen of England', and this omission had caused the most Catholic prince of them all to take serious umbrage. As the widower of Queen Mary Tudor, Philip of Spain had always considered himself something of an expert on English affairs – 'I believe I could give a better opinion upon them and the course that ought to have been adopted under the circumstances than anyone else.' But His Holiness had allowed himself to be carried away by zeal, and Philip feared this 'sudden and unexpected step' would merely serve to exacerbate national feeling and 'drive the Queen and her friends the more to oppress and persecute the few good Catholics still remaining in England.' The majority of the 'moderate sort' of English Catholics fully shared King Philip's disapproval of the Pope's sudden access of zeal, foreseeing that 'thereby a great heap of mischiefs hung over their heads'; while the European hierarchy regretted not so much the excommunication as the fact that the bull had been published without any possibility of putting its provisions into effect. As the Bishop of Padua presently remarked to the Cardinal of Como, there was not much to be gained by turning the key of Peter with one hand unless the other wielded the sword of Paul. By thus resorting to sanctions which he was powerless to enforce, Pius V appeared to his contemporaries to have committed a political blunder of unusual proportions; he had done nothing to improve the already sorry state of Catholicism in England while at the same time damaging the prestige and credibility of the papacy. Indeed, so inept and ill timed was the gesture that there is a school of Catholic thought ready to maintain that it was all a deliberate and dastardly ploy dreamed up by William Cecil, using Roberto Ridolfi to feed the Holy Father with false information designed to persuade him that the northern Catholics needed only a word of encouragement from Rome to undertake the successful overthrow of the heretical regime in London.

The suggestion that the Pope had been enticed by malice aforethought on the part of the English Secretary of State into taking action calculated to injure his own cause seems characterized rather more by imaginative ingenuity than serious probability, although it is true that it was Ridolfi who first introduced a copy of *Regnans in Excelsis* into England and who, according to his own account, arranged to have it nailed to the Bishop of London's door at a time when he would have known very well that it was likely to do more harm than good. Actually, the Vatican, an institution not normally noted for the speed of its reactions had, on this occasion, moved with commendable despatch, but an appeal for help from the Earls of Westmorland and Northumberland, sent off in November 1569, did not arrive in Rome until February, far too late for any meaningful intervention by the Church. Whether deliberately engineered or not, the whole excommunication fiasco had been bedevilled by confusion, misunderstanding and bad intelligence – if Ridolfi had indeed been guilty of peddling false information, he was by no means the only culprit. 'Newsletters' coming out of Germany and the Netherlands that winter stated confidently that the Duke of Norfolk (mysteriously metamorphosed into the Earl of Suffolk) was already married to the Queen of Scots; that an insurgent army more than twenty thousand strong was in the field; that there were disturbances in Wales and Ireland and 'opinion prevailed' that the English would soon 'with one accord declare themselves for the Catholic faith.' The Pope had himself sent a secret emissary to England in the summer of 1569 to sound out the feelings of the native Catholics, and he apparently brought back an encouraging report while, as late as mid-February 1570, Nicholas Sander, a leader of the English Catholic expatriate community in Louvain, was assuring His Holiness that if the papacy would only come out and make a stand, England would shortly be restored to the Roman fold.

By its uncompromising declaration that orthodox Catholicism and allegiance to the Queen were no longer compatible, *Regnans in Excelsis* had given Elizabeth an excellent excuse for treating all her Catholic subjects as potential traitors but, apart from an inevitable hardening of sectarian attitudes and of Protestant suspicions that 'some monster was a-breeding' in the recesses of the Vatican, there was no immediate stepping up of punitive measures against religious dissidents. Instead, in June the Queen issued a meant-to-be-reassuring public statement read in the Star Chamber by Lord Keeper Nicholas Bacon promising that as long as her loving subjects obeyed the law by coming to church on Sundays, she would not allow any of them to be 'molested by an inquisition or examination of their consciences in causes of religion.'

Also that June the Duke of Norfolk, who had been agitating to be let out of the Tower since February, made a voluntary formal submission to the Queen, binding himself on his allegiance utterly to renounce all thought of a marriage to the Queen of Scots and, further, never again to deal in any other cause connected with her but only as his sovereign should command him. This solemn undertaking, as would later emerge, was worth no more than the paper it was written on, but it achieved its desired objective and in August his grace was given leave to return to his London house in Charterhouse Lane on the site of the old Carthusian monastery, where he was ordered to remain still under the nominal supervision of Sir Henry Neville, his custodian in the Tower. The Queen of Scots herself, who had been unceremoniously hurried out of reach of possible rescue attempts in the alarms of the previous winter, was now back in the relatively open surroundings of Chatsworth, the great mansion built by her hostess the Countess of Shrewsbury during the 1550s and 1560s. It seems that having been assured that *Regnans in Excelsis* was in fact 'a vain crack of words that made a noise only', a gesture made on papal initiative alone and not the prelude to the much-dreaded league of Catholic powers, the Queen of England was prepared to take a more relaxed view of both Norfolk and Mary. She had indeed already embarked on another round of negotiations with the Scots aimed at finding a solution to the problem of their former Queen. These talks continued throughout the summer of 1570 with every appearance of serious intent on Elizabeth's part, although Maitland of Lethington was probably not far wrong when he told the Bishop of Ross in August that he did not believe the Queen of England would ever willingly let her cousin go free. Certainly, the ruling Scottish junta had not the least desire to see Mary restored to their midst and a delegation reaching London towards the end of February 1571 made it clear that they would only consider her return in the capacity of Queen Mother to the child King James. They had no authority, they said, to treat on any other basis and asked to return home for further consultation with the Scottish estates. Elizabeth acquiesced, on the understanding that they would obtain fresh powers enabling them 'to treat for a perfect agreement for the full restitution of her majesty', and be back in England within two months ready to proceed. No one, however, was deceived and, in any case, within two months the English government was hot on the track of a major conspiracy involving the Queen of Scots which would effectively put a stop to all talk of her restitution for the foreseeable future.

At just about the time when the Scottish negotiations were aborting, Roberto Ridolfi had notified his intention of returning to Italy on private business, at the same time 'pretending in fair language to be a good servant to the Queen's Majesty and this state.' And so, recorded William Cecil, or Lord Burghley as he had recently become,

> upon great suit moved, he [Ridolfi] came to her Majesty's speech at Greenwich openly in the garden upon our Lady day . . . being Sunday, when he did in like sort make profession of great affection to serve her Majesty and this crown, and to take his leave.

A few days later he was granted a very favourable passport under the Queen's own hand, together with a licence to export two horses or geldings.

Unfortunately, however, it soon appeared that Signor Ridolfi's business abroad was hardly calculated to serve the interests of the Queen of England or her crown. On 10 March Guerau de Spes had informed King Philip that the Queen of Scotland, the Duke of

21

Norfolk and the leaders of the English Catholics were 'wisely resolved' to send an emissary to Spain, who would also see the Duke of Alva in Belgium. On 25 March, the very day on which, according to Lord Burghley, Ridolfi was enjoying a chat with the Queen in the gardens at Greenwich, de Spes was again writing to Philip to tell him that

> the Queen of Scotland and the Duke of Norfolk, in the name of many other lords and gentlemen who are attached to your Majesty's interests and the promotion of the Catholic religion, are sending Rodolfo [*sic*] Ridolfi, a Florentine gentleman, to offer their services to your Majesty, and represent to you that the time is now ripe to take a step of great benefit to Christianity as in detail Ridolfi will set forth to your Majesty.

Ridolfi, it seemed, would carry a letter of credence from the Duke of Norfolk which, as a precautionary measure, had been written in cipher, the key to which de Spes was sending to the King's secretary, Gabriel de Zayas. Also on 25 March the ambassador wrote to Zayas introducing Ridolfi as 'a person of great truth and virtue, and an intimate friend of mine' and urging the secretary to 'favour and forward' him to the best of his ability. It was especially important that the Italian should have an audience with Philip in circumstances of 'the utmost secrecy'.

Ridolfi left England in the last week of March and made straight for Brussels. Approximately two weeks later a young man called Charles Bailly, making the same journey in reverse, provided the emergent English secret service with its first important catch. Bailly, who is variously described as a Scot, a Fleming or a Burgundian, was an educated man speaking several languages who had entered the Queen of Scots' service in 1564 but in 1571 was employed by the Bishop of Ross as a secretary-cum-courier. He was returning from one of Ross's errands when he landed at Dover on or about 12 April, apparently expecting to be able to bribe his way past the customs. Unfortunately, however, there had recently been a spate of rumours of impending danger coming both from Spain and the English refugees in the Netherlands and a special watch was being kept at the Channel ports. Bailly, travelling without a passport, was arrested as a suspicious character and when a search of his baggage revealed a consignment of banned books together with several packets of letters addressed to the Bishop of Ross, he was sent up to

London to be further examined by Lord Cobham, Warden of the Cinque Ports.

Despite every effort to discourage it on the part of the English government, there was a steady traffic in smuggled Catholic books – some works of devotion but most propaganda tracts, pamphlets and broadsheets printed at Louvain, Antwerp and other centres in the Spanish Netherlands. Charles Bailly was carrying a number of copies of *A Defence of the Queen of Scots and the Duke of Norfolk, provoked by a hostile Discourse touching their Pretended Match written by Francis Walsingham*. The discovery of the books was embarrassing for Ross, especially as this was a title he had been caught trying to have printed at an underground press in London the year before, but the letters were a far more serious matter. According to the statement made later by Lord Cobham, when they were first produced for inspection at his house at Blackfriars, his brother Thomas besought him 'with all earnestness, even kneeling on his knees and weeping' that the letters should not be handed over to the authorities, for they would be the undoing of the Duke of Norfolk, of himself and many of their friends.

After some hesitation, Cobham yielded to the importunity of his 'unhappy brother' and went off to the Court to deliver the books to Lord Burghley without mentioning any letters – despite the fact that he was actually carrying the most important of the packets in his pocket at the time. On the following day he sealed up all the letters with his own seal of arms and had them carried round to the Bishop of Ross, with the proviso that they were to be opened only in his presence. It was agreed that there should be a meeting for this purpose at the house of Francis Barty, another of the Bishop's aides, and Ross opened and displayed ciphered letters from survivors of the Northern Rising – notably the Countess of Northumberland and the Earl of Westmorland – who had managed to escape to Flanders; from Francis Englefield, a prominent English Catholic exile, and letters 'superscribed in cipher' which the Bishop said were for the Spanish ambassador and which he promised to read before sending them on. There were other letters, from Roberto Ridolfi, also in code, which Ross put on one side, saying 'These I cannot decipher' and which Cobham thought were the really important ones, the ones sent to the Duke of Norfolk. In this he was quite right, and over the next few weeks official attention would be grimly concentrated on the secret messages from Ridolfi which the

23

government had reason to believe had been carried by Charles Bailly. The day after receiving the books from Lord Cobham, Burghley gave the first indication that his intelligence service had warned him of the existence of a more dangerous cargo than a mere routine parcel of propaganda pamphlets. He had heard 'there were also certain packets of letters brought with the books', he told Cobham, and desired that they might also be sent to him.

CHAPTER TWO

Certain money in gold to be conveyed into Scotland . . .

———◆———

The patient unscrambling of the Ridolfi Plot was to occupy a good deal of Lord Burghley's time and attention during the course of 1571 – beginning with the letters brought over by Charles Bailly. The Spanish ambassador believed it had been 'a most extraordinary piece of good fortune' to save the packet entrusted to Carlos (Bailly) by Ridolfi. In a report dated three months later, de Spes claimed the credit for organizing the recovery of the letters and the alphabet, or key, to the cipher with the help of Thomas Cobham before Lord Burghley heard about them. Another packet was made up with the same cipher characters and, wrote de Spes gleefully, 'Burghley has had a secretary at work upon it for days . . . but without effect, for there is nothing in it.' The actual concocting of the false packet was the work of the Bishop of Ross, who collected a number of old letters together 'to make thereby a like packet as the true packet was, which was sent to the Lord Burghley to content him therewith, as though he had the true packet.' Lord Burghley was not, however, content or deceived for long, if at all. In his official report he refers merely to having been 'abused' by having a packet of forged letters delivered to him.

Bailly, meanwhile, had been committed to the Marshalsea prison, where he was being given every opportunity to communicate with his friends outside through the kind offices of a fellow prisoner and stool pigeon named William Herle – a denizen of that alternative society which lay only just beneath the surface of prosperous Elizabethan life. Here, in the taverns and gambling dens, bawdy houses and squalid back alleys of the great capital city, men of 'broken fortunes', discharged soldiers, drop-outs and debtors and the black sheep of respectable families rubbed shoulders with bully boys and con men, petty crooks and professional killers. It was from the upper ranks of this criminal underclass that the government drew many of its informants, spies, secret agents and *agents provocateurs*, and William Herle appears to have been a fairly typical specimen of the genre. Constantly on the run from his creditors, he had dabbled in piracy among other things, but he claimed distant kinship with the Cecil family and in the spring of 1571 his distinguished relative found a use for him. He was to make friends with Charles Bailly, gain his confidence, supply him with pen and paper, act as postman and report regularly to Lord Burghley.

Charles, whom Herle describes as being 'fearful, full of words, [vain] glorious, and given to the cup', proved fatally unsuspicious and was soon corresponding with the Bishop of Ross, assuring him that 'seeing you have the letter of Ridolfi, I have no fear at all, specially for that you assure me that you have in safety the deciphering.' In this, endorsed by Burghley as 'Charles's first letter to the Bishop of Ross' and dated 20 April, Bailly proceeded to render a careful account of his mission to Flanders: how he had gone in search of the Prior of the Carthusians in Bruges and come up with him on the road to Antwerp; how he had seen and talked to Sir Francis Englefield in a nunnery half a league from Antwerp 'as secretly that I think not two of his servants did see me.' On Englefield's advice, he had gone on to Brussels to try and sort out some problems which had arisen concerning the printing of books for the English Catholic market, stopping on the way at Mechlin, where he had talked to the Countess of Northumberland and some other refugees from the Northern Rising, before returning with the books from Louvain 'the secretliest that I could'. Notwithstanding all this, Charles was not afraid of appearing before the Council to be examined, 'for I promise you, they shall have nothing of me, and I will confess nothing, let them allege to me whatsoever they will, and though they should pluck me in a Hundred Pieces.'

Bailly's first encounter with Lord Burghley took place shortly after this letter was written and was brief and inconclusive, but the pressure on him was mounting. William Herle had assured his employers that Charles was one of the 'secretest ministers' of Ross and the Queen of Scots; that he had been 'a practiser in all their ill dealings in Flanders and that way these three years', and was privy to a 'whole mass of their secrets'. Burghley certainly believed Charles knew a lot more than he was letting on, and at their next interview threatened the prisoner with the loss of his head and/or both his ears. 'It seems he will not believe anything I say', wrote Charles pathetically on 26 April, adding that orders had been given to keep him more closely confined than ever. He begged Ross to help him, for he would rather lose his life than lose his ears.

While the unhappy Charles, his earlier brave words forgotten, prayed to God for deliverance, William Herle was busy tightening the psychological screws, paying late night visits to the prisoner in his cell, or at what he described as 'a secret hole' – presumably a spy hole or chink in the wall – 'sometimes approaching, and sometimes starting aside as one in great fear to be surprised – hazarding my life, as it were, for his comfort and aid.' The point of these artistic performances, of course, being to add 'such causes of . . . dread to him (for that he is fearful beyond measure) as may work him the more to any purpose intended.'

Charles had by this time begun to suspect that 'maistre Erle' was not entirely to be trusted. He was afraid his letters to Ross were not reaching their destination, for the Bishop had never taken up any of his suggestions for alternative postal arrangements. For example, immediately beneath his prison cell there was 'a little house of some poor man' with a gap in the ceiling 'that cometh to my chamber, wherein I may easily thrust my hand'. It should be a simple matter for one of Ross's servants to scrape an acquaintance with the 'poor man', and letters could then be exchanged via this convenient aperture. Better still, messages could have been passed by word of mouth from Bailly's window which gave on to the street and letters hauled up on a string or dropped into waiting hands. Curiously enough, none of these obvious methods of communication ever seem to have been attempted, and William Herle continued to control all incoming and outgoing correspondence.

Charles had been in the Marshalsea for about ten days when Burghley decided it was time to stop playing games, having conceived some suspicion that Ross's courier 'had some greater matter in charge' than the bringing in of banned books. The official report continues,

And so, after Charles had sent 4 or 5 small letters to the Bishop and had received as many or more, all which, written in cipher, were intercepted, it was thought good suddenly to attach Charles and cause him to decipher these letters, for that as they passed there were true copies kept of some of them.

Charles was therefore transferred to the Tower on, probably, 26 April, and a warrant obtained from the Privy Council authorizing the examination of the prisoner 'by all good means', with especial reference to the letters written from the Marshalsea. If he proved difficult, his interrogators were further authorized to threaten him with the rack, 'and as cause shall be given, afterward with some pain of the said torture, procure him to confess the truth.'

A few days later, in a letter to Ross dated, or rather endorsed by an official hand, 29 April, Charles described how he had been taken before Lord Burghley in the early hours – 'this morning before 5 o'clock'; how his lordship had told him that Ross was making daily applications for his release, which the authorities would be glad to concede, but not until Charles had provided the key, or 'alphabet', to the cipher he had used in writing to the Bishop. Burghley was also interested in any letters or verbal messages which he had conveyed to and from the English refugees overseas, notably the Countess of Northumberland, and made it clear that the government meant to extract a confession 'par force ou par amitie'. Burghley evidently felt that force was likely to prove more productive and Charles appears to have been given a taste of the rack later that same day – an experience which left him 'scarce able to go' and 'as pale as ashes'. He begged Ross piteously to save him, or at least not to let them put him again on the rack, 'or I shall be lost for ever.'

His resistance had, in fact, been broken, and on 2 May he signed a letter of submission to Burghley, beginning with an offer to betray his former master's secrets:

> if I might return with mine Honour and Credit unto my Lord the Bishop of Ross, I should be able to advertise you secretly of all their enterprise, and of the Authors, as I have told you, by deciphering the first Letters that Ridolfi shall write unto him, the which shall be very shortly.

He went on to tell of meeting Ridolfi in Brussels,

> who knowing that I pertained to the Bishop of Ross, and understanding of my return hither, stayed me one day more at Bruxells, to help him write certain letters, two whereof were directed to two Lords of this realm, advertising them of his safe arrival on that side.

It appeared that Ridolfi had brought certain 'Instructions' from England to show the Duke of Alva. He had been summoned to the great man's presence and, according to Ridolfi, very favourably received. The 'Instructions' had been discussed in detail and it was clear from Charles's account that they concerned no less a matter than an invasion of England. Alva had asked about the situation of a suitable port for landing his forces, and 'if there were any strong place between London and the port to impeach their coming to London.' Ridolfi told Charles that, although he had been given no 'resolute answer', the Duke had commanded him to go and see the Pope and the King of Spain, both of whom would give him a warm welcome, and had promised that on his return he should receive all the aid and assistance he required.

In the circumstances, the identities of the 'two Lords of this realm', became a matter of pressing interest. Charles could only say that they had been addressed 'one to the number 30 and the other to 40'. In a second statement, dated 5 May, he repeated that Ridolfi had sought him out in Brussels to enlist his help in writing (that is, encoding) and delivering two or three letters for the Bishop of Ross. The letters to 30 and 40, announcing his safe arrival and reporting on his audience with Alva, with a promise to write again from Rome, had contained twenty-five or thirty lines apiece. The one to Ross was shorter, perhaps eight or ten lines, and was little more than a covering note.

Charles also repeated his plea to be allowed to return to his employment with Ross, 'who is wont to use me for the deciphering of such letters as come to him in the French tongue', so that he might 'from day to day give you intelligence of all that cometh to my knowledge, wherein I assure you I would employ myself without asking any recompense.'

Burghley says that 'after much ado' Charles had been induced to reveal the secret of the code used in his correspondence with Ross from the Marshalsea (although, since this code had been passed on to him via William Herle, it seems probable that his lordship was prudently protecting his agent's cover), and that by this means the existence of Ridolfi's letters was discovered.

It was plainly high time for the Bishop of Ross himself to be brought within the scope of the inquiry – a development which that astute and experienced individual was no doubt expecting. Ross had been doing what he could to rescue the unfortunate Charles Bailly, complaining fluently about the cruel, terrible and undiplomatic practice of arresting ambassadors' servants and forcing them, under torture, to reveal their masters' secrets; but he can have had little doubt that Charles's resistance would soon be broken and he had taken the precaution of sending his confidential secretary, one John Cuthbert, who had charge of all his 'secret writings and ciphers', out of the country while the going was still good. He had then taken to his bed with a convenient attack of ague and was still 'bedfast' and feverish when he received a visit from a deputation of Privy Councillors: the Earl of Sussex, Lord Burghley, Sir Walter Mildmay and Sir Ralph Sadler.

Ross admitted sending Bailly to collect copies of the book 'concerning the Queen of Scots' title and the Defence of her Honour' from the Louvain printers. He admitted corresponding with Francis Englefield, with the Countess of Northumberland and John Hamilton who was the Queen of Scots' unofficial agent in the Netherlands, but denied writing any letters to any of the northern rebels. As for Ridolfi, it was true that he had taken letters from the Queen of Scots to the Duke of Alva, to the Pope and the King of Spain but these were all to ask for help against her own rebels – to Alva 'to have aid and support of men to come into Scotland, to land at Dumbarton, or at Leith'; and to the Pope to ask for money to pay for this force. Ridolfi had also been authorized to solicit the Holy Father for reimbursement of 'certain money' which he had already advanced for Mary's cause and which the Pope had promised but not yet paid. Ross agreed that Ridolfi had written to him from Brussels in cipher and agreed, but more reluctantly, that there had been other letters in the packet. Pressed to reveal the identities of the addresses, he hesitated but finally disclosed that 40 was the Queen of Scots and 30 the Spanish ambassador.

The Bishop's papers were searched and a manuscript copy of the *A Defence of the Queen of Scots* confiscated, but thanks to Ross's sensible habit of burning all his ciphered correspondence, nothing else of interest came to light. Asked why, if they really contained 'no other thing but request of aid for money and power against the Queen of Scots' rebels', he went to the trouble of destroying such letters, he replied coolly that he had been afraid Queen Elizabeth might have misunderstood his mistress's motives in seeking help from abroad. Burghley and his colleagues were far from satisfied and it was decided to take the smooth-talking prelate out of circulation for the time being. Ross was therefore placed in the custody of the Bishop of Ely, in whose charge he was to remain throughout the summer, and the Earl of Shrewsbury was instructed to tell the Queen of Scots that, in view of his 'sundry practices' with the English Catholic expatriates and rebels in the Netherlands, Ross was no longer acceptable as an ambassador for any prince professing friendship to the English Queen.

And what of Mary herself? It was fortunate – or unfortunate, according to point of view – that Dumbarton Castle, long held by the remnants of the Marian party in Scotland, should finally have fallen to the government forces at the beginning of April 1571 and that documents found in the castle and thoughtfully passed on to the English authorities by the current Regent Lennox, provided the first authentic evidence of the extent of Mary's relations with the Duke of Alva. But it was the extent of her relations with Roberto Ridolfi which chiefly interested the English government in the spring of 1571, and Shrewsbury was to interrogate his charge 'speedily . . . before any messenger can come from the Bishop of Ross.' She was to be asked for full details of her correspondence with the Italian – what letters she had sent by him or to him, what letters she had received from him. She was to be asked to reveal 'in what manner of cipher Ridolfi did write to her', and whether she was named by the figures of 30 or 40 in any cipher known to her and the Bishop of Ross. Most importantly, Shrewsbury was to say nothing about the answers already given by the Bishop until Mary had, as Burghley fully expected she would, 'fully denied all'.

The Queen of Scots did not disappoint these expectations. She had not written any letters to any person or persons for any purpose to be carried by anyone called Ridolfi. She had never received any letters from Ridolfi at any time in cipher or otherwise, nor did she know of any cipher in which she was named as either 30 or 40. She did not deny writing to certain foreign princes to ask for help against her own rebels – something she felt fully entitled to do since there was apparently going to be no assistance forthcoming from the Queen of England. She refused to give details of these appeals, but insisted they contained nothing prejudicial to Elizabeth or her realm and was sure the Bishop of Ross had at no time practised anything against the Queen's Majesty. Shrewsbury reported that he did not think she had received any intelligence from the Bishop, although her people were 'daily abroad in every corner to learn some news.'

Lord Burghley did not trust the Queen of Scots any more than he trusted the Bishop of Ross or the Spanish ambassador, who also vigorously denied that he was either 30 or 40 in the Ridolfi code, but in spite of a steady flow of alarming rumours being reported by 'secret intelligence' out of Flanders, where it seemed the English Catholic refugees were expecting to be restored to their 'former estates' before the end of the summer, the English end of the inquiry had temporarily run out of steam. Across the Channel, however, the activities of Roberto Ridolfi were beginning to give Queen Elizabeth's government serious cause for concern.

Ridolfi left Brussels for Rome early in May on the second leg of his great sales-promotion tour and, as expected, received a warm welcome from the Pope, to whom he presented his letters of credence. These included one apparently written by the Queen of Scots dated in February, recommending him as a trustworthy messenger who would explain the present condition of her affairs and how urgently she stood in need of the Holy Father's benevolence, aid and paternal favour. As well as his famous 'Instructions', Ridolfi also carried a letter over the Duke of Norfolk's name authorizing him to ask for the Holy Father's benevolence, his moral support and financial assistance for a Catholic expeditionary task force commanded by the Duke of Alva which was to land at the east-coast port of Harwich, where it would be joined by an enthusiastic army of native Catholics, at least 20,000 strong, commanded by Norfolk himself. Ridolfi was to impress the Pope with the strength and size of the English Catholic party and their impatience to overthrow the heretical, schismatic and oppressive regime of Elizabeth Tudor – he could even produce a list of those members of the nobility committed to the cause. All that was needed was just a little help from abroad and the success of the enterprise would be assured. The Queen of Scotland would be rescued from her enemies and joined in marriage with the Duke of Norfolk; 'the ancient laws and the true Christian and Catholic religion' re-established, and the island of England united under the rule of a lawful prince – i.e. Mary Stewart. The fate envisaged for Elizabeth was not spelt out but the life expectancy of any monarch deposed in such circumstances would, of course, be measurable in days, if not hours.

The Pope, whose grasp of English political realities remained tenuous, who knew little of Ridolfi and less of Norfolk, was delighted with the talkative Italian, who came so well recommended and brought him just the sort of news he wanted to hear. He therefore wrote a kind letter to the Queen of Scots and another to the King of Spain, to be delivered in person by 'our dear son Roberto Ridolfi' in whom Philip was implored to repose unhesitating faith, hoping that His Majesty would see his way to furthering an enterprise plainly designed to promote the honour and glory of God. The Spanish ambassador to the Holy See also wrote urging the King 'to accord a very gracious audience to this Ridolfi', for if he ever returned to England he would be useful 'in giving good testimony to the Queen of Scotland and the Catholics of the goodwill your Majesty bears towards their cause.'

Philip's goodwill towards the English Catholic cause was always a crucial factor. The Pope could provide blessings, absolution and moral support for a crusade. He might even provide some cash. But no soldiers would embark at the Flemish ports to cross the North Sea without the King of Spain's command. The King of Spain, therefore, was worthy of Ridolfi's best persuasive efforts, and Ridolfi's best efforts were highly persuasive. Seldom or never, he told Philip, did such an opportunity befall a Christian prince to store up treasure in heaven by doing God's work on earth at so little cost to himself. There were vast numbers of Englishmen not yet abandoned by the grace of God who loathed the lives they were being forced to lead. They could no longer endure the unjust laws, the perfidy, the welter of schism and heresy which prevailed in their country. The self-styled Queen was already distraught, a prey to terror and vacillation. It would all be so easy. The English ports were open and undefended. The Queen of Scots' party was great and powerful. The insurgent nobility were the greatest and most powerful in the land and were ready to lead the way. They were only asking for a supporting force – a few men, a few arms, a little money. The Queen of Scots would be grateful for ever and would use her influence to prevent any future trouble with France. She would also be willing to send her son to Spain to be brought up a Catholic under Philip's eye. In any case, quite apart from the material benefits which would accrue, what work could be more just and acceptable to God than to defend a widow, aid a child and succour the oppressed?

Philip, cautious at first, became gradually more enthusiastic and before the end of July Ridolfi was writing expansive letters to Mary and Norfolk to tell them that the business was as good as settled. The spoilsport in the game of let's pretend being played in Rome and Madrid that summer was the Duke of Alva, who placed no reliance whatever on the English Catholics and could see himself with horrid clarity being forced to take part in a disastrous fiasco. Ridolfi he considered to be a windbag and a fool: 'A man like this, who is no soldier, who has never witnessed a campaign in his life, thinks that armies can be poured out of the air, or kept up one's sleeve, and he will do with them whatever fancy suggests.' Alva had all the professional soldier's natural contempt for ignorant civilians presuming to teach him his business, but at the same time he tried conscientiously to point out to Philip some of the more obvious calamities likely to result 'if we embarked on this affair and failed to bring it to a successful conclusion.' Not merely would Spain be encumbered by the embarrassment and expense of attempting to wage an impossibly difficult war – an embarrassment which her many enemies would not hesitate to exploit – but the cause of religion in the Low Countries would suffer a terminal collapse, while in England itself the Queen of Scots, who represented Catholicism's best, if not only, hope for the future, would certainly be the first to be sacrificed in the event of a failed invasion.

But despite his freely expressed misgivings, Alva was still only a subordinate and in the last resort would have to obey orders from on high. Even bearing in mind that the plan was not to mount an invasion with a view to conquest but to provide a back-up expedition for a 'spontaneous' national rising, he could see that Ridolfi's original estimate of 6,000 men to be landed at Harwich was hopelessly inadequate. If the venture was to have any chance of success a sufficient force would have to be sent to establish the Queen of Scots on the throne; speed would be of the essence and surprise a vital factor. A good deal had been said about the need for secrecy by those in the know in both Italy and Spain, and Alva in particular dreaded the effects of premature disclosure. Ridolfi he had already dismissed as a blabbermouth and he reposed very little confidence in the discretion of Guerau de Spes in London, whom he warned to burn any possibly incriminating documents in his possession. 'If the matter is discovered', he wrote, 'they [the English] will arrest him and take all his papers, and it is better they should find nothing.'

In Alva's opinion, far too much was being committed to paper. He was obliged to forward on to de Spes a packet of letters from Philip to Norfolk, to Mary and the Bishop of Ross, together with letters and lists of instructions from Ridolfi, but he took the precaution of ordering the ambassador to hold on to the letters for the Queen, the Duke and the Bishop and on no account to 'breathe the least word about them' until he received further orders from the King. But though Alva did his best to plug the leaks, he got small thanks for it – de Spes grumbling bitterly about the delay in the dispatches to Spain. 'If the opportunity is lost this year I fear that the false religion will prevail in this island in a way that will make it a harsh neighbour for the Netherlands.'

There was, needless to say, never the slightest realistic chance of keeping the projected expedition a secret. Even without the confessions of Charles Bailly, there were too many interested pairs of eyes and ears marking Ridolfi's progress round Europe and by midsummer enough information was coming in to enable the English government to guess pretty accurately what was in the wind. Then Ridolfi paid a call on the Grand Duke of Tuscany and told him, quite gratuitously about his plans. The Grand Duke at once passed the news back to Queen Elizabeth. But nothing, it seemed, could put a damper on the enthusiasm of Guerau de Spes: 'The suspicions entertained here about the voyage of Ridolfi and his arrival in Rome need not trouble us much' he wrote on 8 August. The English, after all, had been told by Charles that Ridolfi was going to ask for money for Scotland, 'and it does not matter much what they suspect, since the blow will be struck without leaving them time for thought.'

In fact, in London there had been much time for thought 'upon doubt of some great trouble both inward and beyond the seas', and some members of the Council had tried to persuade the Queen to cancel, or at least to curtail her annual summer progress. But Elizabeth insisted, although she did stay in the vicinity of the capital, and on St Bartholomew's Day – that is, 24 August – she was staying at Audley End, the Duke of Norfolk's Essex mansion. Here great efforts were made by the household to persuade Her Majesty to restore the Duke to his 'full liberty'. 'Whereunto', according to Lord Burghley's report,

> her Majesty seemed to give favourable ear, specially upon asseverations that it was thought that he would become a good subject

35

and that he had forsaken the matter of the Queen of Scots and that he was not then suspected of her Majesty to be any of the two Lords ciphered with 30 and 40.

Less than a week later the government finally got the break they needed to crack the Ridolfi affair:

> Even then was it found by a good hap that he [Norfolk] had sent towards Banister his man, being in Shropshire, certain money in gold to be conveyed into Scotland . . . . Upon the taking of this money and sundry letters therewith, whereof some were in cipher and some out of cipher, by those that were out of cipher it was first found that one Higford, the Duke of Norfolk's secretary, had written to Banister at the same time, and that it was likely that he was privy to the ciphered letters. Whereupon the 30 or 31 of August, he was taken from the Duke without his knowledge, and being straitly examined he confessed the whole; that the Duke his master had sent the money, and so forth as in his confession.

The discovery of this money – £600 in gold which was being sent to Laurence Banister, bailiff of Norfolk's northern estates, for transfer on to Mary's surviving partisans in Scotland – does seem to have been the result of a lucky accident. The gold, in a sealed bag, had been entrusted to one Thomas Brown, draper, of Shrewsbury, who was told that he was carrying £50 in silver. But Brown became suspicious, opened the bag and discovered not only gold coin but a bundle of letters tucked in amongst it and, like an honest citizen, went straight to my Lord Burghley with his find. Another version of the story has it that the good draper took the unopened bag to Lord Keeper Bacon, whose St Albans home lay conveniently close by the road north, and 'disclosed his suspicion so that he might learn what he carried.'

Robert Higford, or Hickford, interrogated in the Tower by Secretary of State Thomas Smith and Dr Thomas Wilson, of the Court of Requests, decoded the letter to Banister as well as he could from memory, adding helpfully that the key to the cipher would be found at Howard House, hidden 'under the mat, hard by the window's side, in the entry towards my lord's bedchamber, where the map of England doth hang.' The £600, half in French crowns and the rest in angels and royals, had come in the first instance from Archbishop James Beaton, the Queen of Scots' representative in Paris, and had been forwarded by the French embassy. The enclosed letters were also from M. de la Mothe, the French ambassador. The French government never denied knowledge of the money – indeed they made a strenuous effort to get it back – but the provenance of the contents of Mr Brown's bag mattered less to the English than the fact that the Duke of Norfolk had been caught in the act of meddling in the Queen of Scots' affairs.

According to Higford, his master had personally instructed him what to write to Banister – how the gold from France was to be sent on to Richard Lowther, receiver of the Duke's rents from the Dacre estates, and from thence conveyed secretly into Scotland to Lord Herries, who in turn would pass it to Maitland of Lethington and Kirkcaldy of Grange, still holding out in Edinburgh Castle. It was the Duke himself who had ordered Higford to tell Thomas Brown that he was carrying £50 in silver for Laurence Banister, and although the secretary swore that he knew of no actually treasonable practices being undertaken by Norfolk, he admitted that His Grace had been in direct correspondence with the Queen of Scots and the Bishop of Ross, as well as with James Beaton and a man named Liggons in Paris regarding 'the state of the Scottish Queen's causes' – and all this despite his solemn assurances that he would never again have anything to do with Mary.

A preliminary search of Howard House had not revealed the key to the Duke's cipher but a coded letter was found in Higford's hiding place and sent on to Burghley on 3 September. The suspicion, later confirmed, that this was from the Queen of Scots herself set alarm bells ringing at Court, and that veteran royal servant and Scottish expert Sir Ralph Sadler was hurriedly summoned to take charge at Howard House. Three days later Norfolk was escorted back to the Tower, 'without any trouble' Sadler reported, apart from the gaping of 'a number of idle rascal people' who followed the little procession through the city. Robert Higford now conveniently 'remembered' that the missing cipher might be concealed under the roof tiles at Howard House, 'but he could not so demonstrate it that any man might find it.' Higford was therefore taken back to Charterhouse Lane under guard and duly retrieved the code book, so cunningly hidden 'as it had not been possible to have found it otherwise than by upripping all the tiles, except one had been well acquainted with the place.' The government investigators were now in a position to decipher the letter found under the mat in the Duke's bedroom. This turned out to have been written by the Queen of Scots to the Bishop of Ross the previous February discussing the ramifications of the Ridolfi plot in full and helpful detail. Mary thought Ridolfi would be the best man to send to Spain but was prepared to leave the final decision to the Duke of Norfolk.

Armed with this further evidence of the Duke's involvement with both Mary and Ridolfi, Sadler, Smith and Wilson once more applied themselves to their 'unpleasant and painful toil'. It was, so Thomas Smith indicated to Lord Burghley on 17 September, a thoroughly distasteful business. Nevertheless, the inquiry was now at last making progress, thanks largely to the several statements of William Barker, Norfolk's other confidential secretary who had joined Robert Higford and Laurence Banister in the Tower. Barker appeared to have played a more active part in the Ridolfi affair than either of his colleagues, although, in the opinion of Thomas Smith, he had been chosen more for his zeal than his wit. It was Barker who had taken delivery of the gold from the French embassy and Barker who had carried letters and messages to and from the Bishop of Ross, who 'was always intimating . . . that the Duke my master should not despair of the marriage with the Queen of Scots', adding that the Earls of Arundel, Derby and Southampton, Lord Montague, Lord Lumley and others were still 'friends of the cause', as well as many other knights and gentlemen.

Barker had not cared for Ridolfi, whom he described as bad-tempered and 'a bitter man', but he had all the same had quite a number of interesting chats with him, in one of which Ridolfi had asked questions about the port of Harwich, whether it were a good haven and did it lie in the Duke's country. One way and another William Barker, in his capacity as errand boy, had had a good deal to do with Ridolfi during the weeks leading up to his departure for the Continent and had been responsible for smuggling the Italian into Howard House. 'I brought him to my Lord in Lent last between eight and nine of the clock . . . and he talked with my lord about three quarters of an hour, and I brought him out of the gate.'

Ridolfi left a paper with the Duke containing a long list of the names of his supposed sympathizers, but according to Barker Norfolk had not looked at it and gave it to him to return to Ridolfi. The Duke had also refused Ridolfi's request for letters of recommendation to the various European potentates he was planning to visit. Ridolfi complained that 'except he had some credit from my Lord, he could do no good', but the Duke stood firm and when the Bishop of Ross 'marvelled' at his refusal, Barker had pointed out that he might consider how dangerous it would be for his master to write that Ridolfi was acting in his name. The pressure, however, had been maintained. Ross and Ridolfi read Barker a document setting out the itinerary of the Italian's projected journey:

> that first he would go to the Duke of Alva, in the Queen of Scots' name and the Duke of Norfolk's name, and desire his help for the Queen of Scots; and that he would go further to solicit the Pope, and the King of Spain, for men and money . . . and that Ridolfi would move the King of Spain to send three or four thousand harquebusiers to invade England, and another force to invade Ireland, that the Queen's majesty's trouble might be the greater.

Barker was to pass all this on to the Duke, and a few days later he had brought Ridolfi to see his master for the second time. The two had talked for about an hour in the gallery of Howard House and afterwards Ridolfi told Barker that 'they were agreed of his journey, and that my Lord prayed him to go on with it.'

From the statements made by Norfolk's secretaries, the Council's investigators heard about the methods used for smuggling correspondence as well as visitors in and out of their master's prisons, of 'writings' cunningly concealed in wine bottles with specially marked corks, or cast into 'a little dark privy house' which had served as a letter box. More importantly, they learnt from William Barker the true identities of '30' and '40'. The former had been Lord Lumley, Norfolk's brother-in-law and close friend, while 40 had been no less a person than the Duke himself.

In his examination on 10 October, Barker provided some interesting supplementary information about the famous '40' letter carried by Charles Bailly and delivered to the Bishop of Ross through the good offices of Lord Cobham. Barker had received this document, duly deciphered, at the hands of John Cuthbert, Ross's now missing secretary, 'in the field where the Windmill doth stand on the back side of the Duke's house', and had taken it to his master, who, according to Barker, had read it aloud in his presence. To the best of his recollection,

> the effect of which letter was, that Ridolfi had spoken with the Duke of Alva . . . and that the Duke did like well of the matter that Ridolfi came for, and willed in any wise that the matter might

be kept secret, and promised to do his best therein; and willed that when a foreign power should enter into this land at the port which Ridolfi had named [that is, Harwich], that the friends to the enterprise here in England, might be in a readiness with force between that port and London, that the power which the Duke of Alva should send might the more safely land and settle themselves, and that Ridolfi would go on in his voyage to solicit the matter further, first to the Pope, and then to the King of Spain.

If this were not damning enough, Barker went on to reveal how, back in the summer of 1570, on the instructions of the Bishop of Ross, he had passed on to the Duke full details of a plan being concocted by a group of Catholic gentlemen – the brothers George and Francis Rolston, Thomas and Edward Stanley, Sir Thomas Gerard and John Hall – to release the Queen of Scots by stealing her away out of a window and convey her to France or Flanders; and how the Duke had said 'it would do very well, and, for his part, thought that Spain would be the surest place for her.' The Queen of Scots had written to him about this scheme, which, of course, came to nothing, and also to the Bishop of Ross.

'About midsummer last', Norfolk had acquired a still more dangerous correspondent, when 'in a packet of letters sent from the Bishop of Glasgow to the Bishop of Ross, there was a letter sent from Ridolfi to the Bishop of Ross, and therein a letter sent from the Pope to the Duke of Norfolk.' The message which had taken this circuitous route was to the effect that though the Pope 'could not this year help the Queen of Scots', she and the Duke should not despair, for the Holy Father would soon find 'a convenient time to relieve her'.

This letter, endorsed with the cipher '40', had, like the others, been decoded by John Cuthbert who 'knew all the secrets touching the Duke and the Scottish Queen.' No wonder the Bishop of Ross had been so anxious to get him out of reach of the English authorities. Throughout the interrogations of Norfolk's servants the Bishop's name had been cropping up with ominous regularity and it was obvious that despite his earlier denials, his lordship was implicated up to his neck in the Ridolfi affair. It was high time he was re-called to account, and accordingly, on 16 October, the Bishop of Ely received instructions to deliver his involuntary house guest back to the authorities. Ross, who had been spending the summer pleasantly enough with his custodian in East Anglia, was brought under escort to London and lodged temporarily with the Lord Mayor.

Accused of double-dealing by a high-powered committee of the Privy Council, Ross pleaded diplomatic immunity. As 'a stranger and a Scottishman' his first loyalty was quite properly to his own prince and country, but throughout the four years of his ambassadorship he had done his best to please the Queen of England by advising the Queen of Scots and her party to agree to such reasonable conditions put forward by the English government which might lead to the recovery of her liberty and 'the common quietness of both these realms'. The English, however, were not impressed. Lord Burghley had taken legal advice on the question of Ross's privileged status and had been informed that any ambassador seeking to procure an insurrection or rebellion in the country to which he was accredited could be held to have forfeited his immunity from prosecution. It was, in short, made brutally clear to the Bishop that neither his cloth nor his ambassadorial dignity would protect him from the rigours of criminal investigation – not excluding 'the pinches or racks' – if he failed to co-operate with his interrogators. He was then removed 'instantly' to the Tower and placed in what he mournfully described as

> a very evil and infected house where no man of honest calling had been kept many years before, with close windows, and doors with many locks and bolts . . . with a cockshot, as they call it, set up without, right against my windows to keep away all light and sight from me.

John Leslie was not the stuff of which heroes and martyrs are made and a very few days of this uncomfortable and disorientating confinement were enough to convince him that further resistance would be pointless as well as unwise. In a series of examinations between the last week of October and the first week of November he told the Privy Council all he knew, which turned out to be pretty much all there was to know about the Ridolfi affair as it had been conducted by himself, the Queen of Scots, the Duke of Norfolk, the Spanish ambassador, the Earl of Arundel, the Lords Cobham and Lumley, not to mention other, more peripheral *dramatis personae* such as the Stanley brothers, Francis Englefield, Francis Barty, a member of his own staff who had been involved with the Cobhams over the hocus-pocus with the letters carried by Charles Bailly, plus

41

various members of the Catholic or crypto-Catholic gentry who had played still more minor parts.

Although Ross does not appear to have given his interrogators any information they had not already extracted from other sources, his statements provided copious corroborative detail which was to prove very valuable in building up the case against Mary and Norfolk. The Bishop wrote to Mary attempting to justify his wholesale betrayal of her trust by saying that since it appeared that her clandestine correspondence with the Duke had already fallen into government hands, whereby 'they were made privy to the most secret matters that your Majesty at any time did treat with him', and since Norfolk and his servants, 'immediately after his last entry to the Tower', had made full confessions and submitted themselves to Queen Elizabeth's clemency, he had really had no choice but to 'plainly and truly declare to the Council the whole proceedings . . . betwixt your Majesty and the Duke.' Ross had also felt impelled to make a clean breast of all the undercover dealings involving Norfolk, Ridolfi, the Pope, the King of Spain and the Duke of Alva – dealings which he now considered to have been vain and impracticable. Indeed, he went so far as to attribute 'this whole discovery' to God's special Providence in preventing Mary from looking to foreign enemies for relief, and showing her instead the better path of patience, Christian resignation and reliance on the wise and kindly guidance of the Queen of England and her councillors. This letter, which was plainly written under super-vision, or at any rate censorship, ended with a plea for money – Ross had been obliged to pay all his own expenses since his arrest more than six months ago and was now seriously out of pocket.

Like so many of those unfortunate enough to become involved in the affairs of the Queen of Scots, John Leslie had been given ample cause to regret it, and there seems no reason to doubt that he was genuinely anxious now to be shot of the whole business. In an extraordinary outburst to Thomas Wilson he declared that the Queen his mistress was not fit for any husband; that he had been credibly informed that she had poisoned her first husband, the French king; that she had consented to the murder of her second; had matched with his murderer, the Earl of Bothwell, and had brought *him* to the field (at Carberry Hill) to be murdered. As for her projected marriage to Norfolk, Ross did not believe she would have long kept faith with him and the Duke would not have had 'the best days with her'! 'Lord, what people are these! What a Queen, and what an Ambassador!' commented Dr Wilson in his report to Burghley on 8 November.

By this time the details of the Ridolfi affair had become public knowledge – the Lord Mayor and aldermen of the city of London having been officially informed about the discovery of a most dangerous conspiracy to overthrow the Protestant religion, dethrone Queen Elizabeth and replace her with Mary Queen of Scots by force of foreign arms, a most dangerous conspiracy which had involved the Pope, the King of Spain and the Duke of Norfolk. Armed with the additional corroboration provided by the Bishop of Ross, the government was now ready to proceed against Norfolk, but first the Queen and Burghley wanted to get rid of Guerau de Spes. The ambassador had from the beginning scarcely troubled to conceal his hostility and contempt for the Protestant court to which he had been accredited and had consistently and actively intrigued to bring about its downfall.

The uncovering of the English end of the Ridolfi affair with the second arrest of the Duke of Norfolk and the confessions of his secretaries had, of course, cut the thread of the whole business, as the King of Spain put it, and neither he or the Duke of Alva can have been exactly surprised to hear in mid-December that de Spes was being given notice to quit for conduct incompatible with his diplomatic status. He huffed and puffed and demanded to be given time to receive instructions from Alva and to settle his affairs in London, but he had to go at little more than a week's notice. And good riddance, indicated the Queen, who told Guido Cavalcanti, the French Queen Mother's agent, that she really did not care whether he was replaced or not. The King of France, she remarked airily, could see how little she cared for the King of Spain by the way she had ordered his ambassador to go without delay – a highhanded attitude made easier by the fact that England had just concluded a comprehensive treaty of friendship with the French.

Norfolk was finally brought to trial before a court of his peers in January 1572, convicted of high treason and sentenced to death. Although the verdict, which was unanimous, had never been in question, the proceedings themselves were no more, possibly rather less, inequitable than any other sixteenth-century political trial, nor did the Duke, in his defence, deny having known something of Ridolfi's plans. He did deny having taken any active part in the

43

plotting, but while he may have retained just enough common sense not to have signed his name to the various documents being handed about by the Italian, there can really be no reasonable doubt that he had been willing to discuss and advise, or that he would have been more than willing to profit by the schemes under discussion. There is no doubt at all that, despite his solemn promises to the contrary, he had continued to correspond with the Queen of Scots, to lend her money and to offer suggestions, not only about Scottish affairs and her plans for escape, but on the terms of the treaty she had been negotiating with Elizabeth. Behind the grand façade of wealth and breeding, Thomas Howard was revealed as having the soul of a small-time crook: weak, greedy and foolish. He had been riding a tiger for the past three years and was lucky to have lasted as long as he did.

Had it all been a put-up job? A trap carefully laid and baited by William Cecil to catch Norfolk and, perhaps, the Queen of Scots herself? It is true that there are some rather suspicious aspects to the affair – for example, the fact that as soon as Ridolfi was safely out of England vital clues began to be scattered like confetti. It is also true that all Ridolfi's activities in Brussels, Rome and Madrid during the spring and summer of 1571 can be made to appear specifically designed to compromise his English confederates. Roberto Ridolfi may or may not have been acting as an *agent provocateur* in the pay of the English secret service. He may very possibly have been serving more than one master. In his line of business he would have been most unusual if he had not been taking, or at the least attempting to take, a rake-off from both sides. This has to remain a matter for speculation, but while the traditional Protestant story of a dastardly Catholic plot should perhaps no longer be swallowed quite whole, there is no doubt that a scheme, however impracticable, to secure foreign Catholic help to release Mary Queen of Scots and over-throw the legally constituted government of the Protestant Queen Elizabeth did exist. Exactly when and to what extent it was penetrated by Lord Burghley and his agents is never likely to come to light. As for the Duke of Norfolk, he may well have been a victim, but he was throughout the victim of his own character defects, his own vanity and lack of any political sense rather than the malice of William Cecil.

Cecil's other presumed target, meanwhile, was flatly denying that she had ever even thought of attempting to stir up rebellion against her good sister and tender cousin. Mary Stewart meant no harm to Elizabeth Tudor despite the fact that, as she pointed out, Elizabeth had supported her rebellious subjects against her, had stood by while they took away the crown from her head and had since done nothing to help restore her to her throne. She had had no dealings with the Duke of Norfolk 'since the time of his restraint'. Although she had at one time genuinely believed that their marriage would have been welcomed by the English people and agreeable to the Queen and Council, Norfolk was Elizabeth's subject and Mary considered herself in no way responsible for his actions or for his present predicament. She also once more denied having had any connection with Ridolfi – 'she never saw him, nor had to do with him' – though she did later admit having given him a financial commission. And so, wrote Ralph Sadler, who was taking the Earl of Shrewsbury's place as Mary's custodian during the latter's absence at the Norfolk trial, 'and so she flyeth from all things which may touch her, and will needs be innocent of all manner of practices tending . . . to the peril of the Queen's majesty, or any other distubance of this State.'

Sadler did not believe her and neither did anybody else who had seen the evidence. Nor is there any reason why she should have been innocent. The Queen of Scots was a 'bonnie fechter', a lioness of the royal breed, as she described herself, a free and sovereign princess who had been unjustly imprisoned by her cousin and rival. Since the promulgation of *Regnans in Excelsis* she had, as a good Catholic, good moral grounds for regarding Elizabeth as a usurper to be resisted by any means available. 'Her letters and discourses . . . being in cypher, to the Duke of Norfolk are found', Burghley had written to the Earl of Shrewsbury after his ferrets had been through Howard House, and Mary was known to have been corresponding also with Guerau de Spes and the Duke of Alva. 'Ah, the poor fool will never cease until she lose her head', remarked her former brother-in-law, the King of France, after reading the reports of his ambassador in London.

But, in spite of everything, there seemed no immediate prospect of such an eventuality. Elizabeth's attitude towards her cousin hardened. She abandoned her policy of negotiation and significantly allowed the Earl of Moray's version of the Darnley affair, together with the much-disputed Casket Letters, to be published for the first time. Mary's household underwent one of its periodic purges and

45

there was a general tightening of security at Chatsworth. But apparently this was as far as the English Queen meant to go. Even the Duke of Norfolk was still alive; three times the warrant for his execution had been signed and three times Elizabeth had revoked it at the last moment. Her well-wishers were in despair at this display of feminine weakness. 'The Queen's Majesty hath been always a merciful lady and by mercy she hath taken more harm than by justice', wrote Burghley to Francis Walsingham, now *en poste* at the English embassy in Paris, after the first of these postponements. 'God's will be fulfilled and aid her Majesty to do herself good', he sighed after the second.

In the end Norfolk had to be sacrificed. The pressure exerted by the Parliament of May 1572 was too strong to be resisted, and at last, reluctantly, the Queen gave in. Norfolk went to the block on 2 June that year, but surprisingly enough, he was the only casualty of the Ridolfi affair. All those members of the aristocracy – the Cobham brothers, Lord Lumley, the Earls of Arundel and Southampton among them – who had been arrested in the general round-up of the previous autumn were let off with a caution and quietly released. Nor did Barker, Banister and Higford suffer the full rigour of the law. William Barker, whose testimony against his master had been so valuable to the authorities, was granted a royal pardon and together with his colleagues disappeared from the record. Charles Bailly, though he claimed to be a broken man as a result of his long and rigorous confinement, was also presently released and allowed to go abroad, as was the Bishop of Ross, on condition that he undertook never again to meddle in the affairs of the Queen of Scots. As for Roberto Ridolfi, he lived on into his eighties, dying at last in his native Florence full of years and honours, although he always maintained that he had suffered serious financial losses as a result of his endeavours to serve the cause of the Catholic Church of England.

But in 1572 the most notable survivor was, of course, the Queen of Scots herself, around whom the whole crazy house of cards had been erected. Considering that evidence could be brought to show that Mary would have welcomed an invading army into England, her survival was a matter of consternation and deep regret to many. A committee of both Houses of Parliament was appointed to discuss the 'great cause' of the Scottish Queen's future, and after hearing its preliminary report, the Commons made it perfectly clear

what they wanted done about her. They wanted to 'cut off her head
and make no more ado about her.' With scarcely a dissenting voice,
the clamour grew for a final solution to the problem of that sower
of sedition and disturber of the peace, that notorious whore and
murderess, that 'monstrous and huge dragon'. 'A general impunity
to commit treason was never permitted to any', declared the
Londoner and literary man Thomas Norton. Another member
could see no reason why the Queen of Scots should not be dealt
with as she deserved. She had come into England not as an enemy,
but worse, as a dissembling friend, and under the guise of friendship
had sought the destruction of the Queen's majesty. 'Shall we say
our law is not able to provide for this mischief? We might then say
it hath defect in the highest degree.'

Parliament in 1572 was not just baying for blood and vengeance.
The knights and burgesses gathered in the Palace of Westminster
that spring could see their whole way of life, their peace and
prosperity, the future peace and prosperity of their children and
grandchildren being put at risk and they were frankly afraid. They
knew what was happening in the religious wars currently ravaging
France and the Low Countries. Enough people living in the south
and east had heard enough first-hand atrocity stories from Dutch,
Flemish and Huguenot refugees to give them good reason to be
afraid – and such stories lost nothing in the telling as they spread
through the population. The prevalent English dread of Popish
plots, of the invading armies of anti-Christ breathing fire and
slaughter, of pillage and rape, famine and persecution, may have
been a touch exaggerated, but they were very understandable, given
the political climate of the time, and speaker after speaker in the
Commons debate made the point that their lives, their lands and
their goods would all be forfeit if ever the Catholic Queen of Scots
succeeded to the throne.

Queen Elizabeth, however, was unmoved by the urgent and
piteous appeals being addressed to her: 'Partly for honour, partly
for conscience, for causes to herself known' she would not agree to
the framing of a Bill of Attainder against Mary and thus, for the
second time, by her own deliberate personal intervention, she saved
the life of the woman she now knew beyond any shadow of doubt
to be her mortal enemy. It was a decision taken in defiance of the
will of the nation as expressed by its elected representatives; against
the combined weight of the House of Lords, the Privy Council, the

Church and the legal profession; against every argument of expediency, prudence and plain common sense – or so it seemed to all reasonable men. But Elizabeth took a cooler view of politics and plots. That April her representatives had signed the draft protocol of the Treaty of Blois, giving her a defensive alliance with France by which both countries undertook to come to the aid of the other if either were attacked by a third party, even on religious grounds, and in which both agreed to work for the pacification of Scotland. Most importantly from the English point of view, it contained no mention of Mary Stewart and no provisions for her welfare. The Treaty of Blois, in fact, marked the final abandonment of Mary's cause by the French government and gave Elizabeth what amounted to a free hand in settling the Scottish question. This was a solid and very valuable diplomatic gain, which the Queen of England had no intention of jeopardizing by proceeding to extremes against her cousin, whatever the provocation. And in any case Elizabeth Tudor intended to play the game of statecraft by her rules, or not at all. She would never, as she repeatedly made clear to her long-suffering councillors, she would never be constrained by anybody to do anything.

But then the Queen was something else – a political genius often relying on instinct, intuition and her own special brand of magic in the conduct of affairs. Lesser mortals, sober, hard-headed, God-fearing men like William Cecil and Francis Walsingham with no such resources to draw on, had to concentrate on the painstaking gathering of intelligence so vital in the unremitting struggle against the forces of anti-Christ, and could not always afford to be over fastidious about the methods used.

CHAPTER THREE

The English harvest

In August 1572 Francis Walsingham had had two years at the embassy in Paris – years largely spent working to negotiate the new Anglo-French alliance. But the Treaty of Blois in its final form was purely defensive and not, as Walsingham and the French Protestant party would have preferred, an offensive league aimed at curbing the growth of Spanish power in the Netherlands. Unfortunately, though, the Huguenots' natural desire to see the Duke of Alva chased out of Flanders was to help to trigger off a massive Catholic backlash which not only put the new-born *entente* at serious risk but served to set in concrete the fears and prejudices of every European Protestant from John Knox's Edinburgh to Calvin's Geneva.

The Massacre of St Bartholomew's Day is one of history's more spectacular horror stories and provides a depressing example of what sectarian hatred can achieve. Ironically enough, the occasion of this particular demonstration was an apparent attempt at reconciliation between the King of France, Charles IX, and his Huguenot subjects, sealed on 18 August by the marriage of the King's sister Marguerite and the Huguenot prince Henry of Navarre. Both reconciliation and marriage had been engineered by the King's mother, that optimistic *politique* Catherine de Medici, who needed allies to play off against the predatory (and ultra-Catholic) Guise family. But Catherine had become seriously disturbed by the influence which the veteran Huguenot leader, Admiral Coligny, was establishing over her neurotic and unstable son, and feared that in his anxiety to relieve the pressure on the Dutch Protestants, Coligny would sooner or later involve Charles in war with Spain.

The Italian Queen Mother, acutely jealous of her hard-won position of power behind the throne, decided with devastating practicality that Coligny must go, confidently entrusting the Guises with the actual task of disposal. This should have taken place on 22 August, but at the crucial moment the Admiral stooped to adjust a slipping overshoe and the assassin's bullet missed its mark, shattering the victim's arm. Greatly shocked, the King sent his own physicians to attend Coligny, came personally to enquire and promised a full investigation into the outrage. His mother, realizing that her own complicity would inevitably be discovered, hastily counter-attacked. She persuaded Charles that his own life was in imminent danger from a Huguenot murder plot and that his only recourse was to sanction the immediate and wholesale killing of the Huguenot notables so conveniently assembled for the Navarre wedding.

Catherine anticipated no difficulty in putting her plan into action. The Parisians were predominantly and hot-temperedly Catholic and the presence of several thousand angry and suspicious Protestants was doing nothing to lower the temperature in the capital. Although the wedding festivities had ended, the streets remained unusually full of people showing an odd reluctance to go back to work, and numbers of armed men could be seen mingling with the crowds.

Across the river in the Faubourg St Germain, Queen Elizabeth's ambassador, his wife and daughter and their guest, Philip Sidney, waited nervously for news. In the small hours of 24 August the distant clamour of church bells may have disturbed a wakeful member of the Walsingham household and later in the morning rumours of a disturbance of some kind near the Louvre began to circulate; but it was not until groups of terrified Protestants, English and other nationalities, came seeking sanctuary at the embassy that Walsingham and his family learnt the full horror of the situation. Those church bells had been the signal for Catholic to fall upon Huguenot, and Paris was like a sacked city, the streets littered with corpses, the very gutters, according to some accounts, running with blood.

That night and all next day the beleaguered occupants of the English embassy remained huddled together in fear, praying for deliverance but expecting to be dragged out and butchered at any moment. They were, in fact, lucky to survive. A mob which has tasted blood is no respecter of diplomatic immunity, and the French government had quickly lost control of the monster it had unleashed. The slaughter spread to the provinces and altogether it is estimated that some ten thousand Huguenots or suspected Huguenots – men, women and children – lost their lives.

European reaction to the news of St Bartholomew varied: Te Deums were sung in Rome, which was illuminated as for a great victory; the Pope ordered commemorative medals to be struck; and the King of Spain sent his personal congratulations to the King of France. The Dutch insurgent leader, William of Orange, on the other hand, declared that Charles would never be able to cleanse himself of the bloody deed, and from distant Russia even Ivan the Terrible was moved to register a protest.

In England, where boatloads of Huguenot refugees were arriving daily in the Channel ports, the French ambassador was dismayed by the strength of the popular feeling which had been stirred up by 'confused rumours' of the events in Paris. The English, he reported sadly, were expressing 'extreme indignation and a marvellous hatred against the French, reproaching loudly broken faith, with great execration of excesses and so many kinds of outrages.' Even after the official version of events in Paris had been conveyed to them, the islanders showed no sign of moderating their opinions. Openly sceptical of tales of Huguenot conspiracies, they preferred to believe 'that it was the Pope and the King of Spain who kindled the fire in France . . . and that there is something evil afoot from all three of them against England.'

News of the death of Admiral Coligny in the general holocaust of Bartholomew's Day had brought a special frisson of dread across the Channel. It was not just that Coligny had been a wounded man trusting to the protection of his King which made his murder so shocking. After the assassination of the Scottish Regent Moray in January 1570, he was the second Protestant leader to die by violence, and fear that 'this barbarous treachery will not cease in France but will reach over unto us' – fear that Queen Elizabeth, on whose life depended the survival of the Protestant state, might become the next victim of an assassin's bullet – continued to prey on the minds of many thoughtful Englishmen. It certainly preyed on the mind of Francis Walsingham. Deeply shaken by his experiences during the massacre, he had been left with a conviction, which he never saw any reason to modify, that it was not possible for Protestants to do business with any of the Catholic powers. 'I think less peril to live with them as enemies than friends', he wrote to the

51

Privy Council on 24 September, just one month after the 'miserable accident' of Bartholomew's Day.

Despite the pressure of public opinion, the ranting of popular preachers and the urging of her more radical advisers, the Queen did not break off diplomatic relations with France, nor did she repudiate the Treaty of Blois. Neither she nor the French government were in a position to indulge in grand gestures of this kind, and were ready enough to help each other smooth over the embarrassment caused by recent unfortunate events. But Francis Walsingham had had enough. He asked to be recalled and at last, after repeated appeals and many piteous references to the wretched state of his health, the worse condition of his finances and the fact that his wife was heavy with child, Elizabeth reluctantly agreed to let him come home. He returned to England in April 1573 and that December was sworn a member of the Privy Council and appointed Principal Secretary of State jointly with Sir Thomas Smith.

Many and various were the duties and responsibilities which fell to the lot of a conscientious Elizabethan Secretary of State, ranging from the handling of matters of international diplomacy at the highest level to settling local disputes over town charters or Oxford colleges. Because of his previous experience – as well as his stint at the embassy in Paris, Walsingham had spent some time on the Continent as a young man – he was regarded as an expert on foreign affairs and dealt routinely with most of the business which would today be regarded as the province of a Foreign Secretary. He also kept an eye on Irish affairs and regularly presented matters on behalf of the Queen to be considered by the Privy Council. But it is as the Queen's spy-master that Francis Walsingham is best remembered – a cold-hearted, ruthless manipulator of the truth, 'a most subtle searcher of hidden secrets', who 'outdid the Jesuits in their own bow and overreached them in their own equivocation.'

This, at least, is the legend. The reality is rather more prosaic. Like so many others of the period, the Walsingham family had risen from trade to join the ranks of the squirearchy and by the time Francis was born, most probably in the year 1532, the process of gentrification was complete, the Walsinghams being comfortably established in north Kent with estates in the neighbourhood of Chislehurst and Footscray. Little, if anything, is known about his early life but his father died when he was still a small child and it seems reasonable to assume that the young Francis first absorbed the teaching of the Protestant faith from his mother and her second husband, both of whom came from families prominent in the reforming movement. He was educated at King's College, Cambridge, at that time a veritable hotbed of advanced Protestantism, and in 1552 enrolled as a member of Gray's Inn – some knowledge of law being considered a desirable qualification for any gentleman and especially for one contemplating a public career.

But young Francis Walsingham was not destined to be called to the Bar. In the following year Edward VI died, Catholic Mary Tudor succeeded, the English political world turned upside down and became potentially decidedly unhealthy for those who, like Francis Walsingham, regarded themselves as professing 'the purer religion'. Many committed Protestants survived the Marian reaction by simply keeping their heads down and their opinions to themselves. Others, unwilling to compromise with their consciences, travelled abroad to more congenial climes, among them, so it would appear, Francis Walsingham. Information about his period of voluntary exile, said to be for the sake of his religion, is extremely sparse. He spent some months in Italy at the University of Padua studying Roman civil law and, quite probably, the maxims of Niccolo Machiavelli, as well as observing at first hand the labyrinthine methods, the guile, the sharp practice and the deliberate trickery employed by the rulers of the small Italian city states in their unremitting struggle for independent survival.

After leaving Padua in the spring of 1556, Walsingham dropped out of sight altogether. He probably lived for a time in France and it certainly seems reasonable to assume that he would have visited his fellow expatriates who had set up godly congregations in Basle, Strasburg and Frankfurt. But this is conjecture. Whether deliberately or not, Francis Walsingham successfully covered his tracks. He was back in England, though, early in 1560, and two years later sat in the second Elizabethan Parliament as member for Lyme Regis. Walsingham was not without useful connections. His mother, Joyce, was the sister of Sir Antony Denny, close friend and servant of Henry VIII and an executor of his will. His step-father, John Carey, was the brother of the Carey who married Mary Boleyn, the Queen's maternal aunt. One of his sisters married Sir Walter Mildmay. But his most influential friend and contact in the political world was undoubtedly William Cecil. Always on the look-out for new talent, Cecil seems to have marked down the solemn, dark-eyed young man with his gift for languages and sound views on religion as a promising candidate for public office, and it was very likely Cecil who arranged his election to the House of Commons. In the autumn of 1566 the Secretary of State made a note to remind himself to ensure that Mr Walsingham was of the House when Parliament met again at the end of September, and by 1568 he was employing Mr Walsingham to undertake a variety of small commissions connected with intelligence and security matters.

When Mr Walsingham stepped into William Cecil's shoes as Secretary himself some five years later, he inherited his predecessor's system of spies and informers which, as witnessed by the Ridolfi affair, had proved a far from inefficient instrument when it came to plot-breaking. It was on these foundations that Francis Walsingham, in addition to his many other responsibilities, built up the formidable and far-reaching intelligence network on which his notoriety depends. He drew his information from a wide range of sources. A good deal of it came in through the normal diplomatic channels. Queen Elizabeth's representatives abroad were all expected to set up their own intelligence services (this was an important part of the job for the ambassadors of every first-rate power), and there was always at least one servant or secretary or minor official to be found in every court or great man's household ready to part with gossip, hearsay, scandal, speculation and sometimes even with hard news if the price was right. Walsingham could also call on the friendly offices of Dutch, French and German Protestant community leaders. In addition to these official and semi-official sources, he made use of a small army of free-lance news-gatherers scattered all over Europe. These included merchants, traders, businessmen, commercial agents, licensed travellers and petty functionaries who would, for a consideration, pass on any interesting items which might happen to come their way.

From a list drawn up after his death, it seems that Walsingham had been in the habit of receiving reports from twelve places in France, nine in Germany, four in Italy (he had even contrived to penetrate the English College at Rome), four in Spain, three in the Low Countries and from as far afield as Constantinople, Algiers and Tripoli. As well as his foreign network, he had four regular agents in England who were engaged in tracking the movements of the Jesuit and other seminary priests – Catholic missionaries who began to infiltrate across the Channel by the mid 1570s. One way and another, it would probably be no exaggeration to say that very little went on in Catholic circles either at home or abroad during the 1570s and 1580s which did not, sooner or later, come to the notice of Francis Walsingham's office.

By today's standards, of course, Queen Elizabeth's famous secret service appears pitifully small and amateurish. There were probably never more than about a dozen full-time professional agents on the pay-roll at any given moment. Trustworthy professional agents, always in short supply, tended to come expensive, and it was not until 1582 that Walsingham began to receive any sort of regular budget for his intelligence work. It started at a grudging £750 per annum and was gradually increased to £2,000 by the crisis year of 1588. When he first took over, most of the cost of developing the secret service is said to have come out of his own pocket. His operatives, both full- and part-time, were a floating population of greatly varying ability and reliability, working individually and working, very often, for both sides. Many of their reports were sheer guesswork, many were very likely sheer invention and the service owed its remarkable record of success to the skill and flair which enabled Francis Walsingham to sort out the mass of seemingly unrelated material which came into his hands, piece it together and make from it a coherent whole. It was a task which demanded not only endless patience and capacity for taking pains, but an instinct for spotting and interpreting the single relevant fact or sentence in an agent's report. Walsingham had the patience and the dedication. He developed the instinct slowly through unremitting hard work and concentration – his vigilance to gather true intelligence was noted by the seventeenth-century editor of his dispatches from France – and he was undoubtedly helped by his deep sense of the righteousness of the cause he served. Sincere religious convictions were, after all, by no means a Catholic monopoly. Walsingham held distinctly radical or fundamentalist religious views which, despite the valuable and devoted services he rendered her, was why the Queen never really liked him. The historian William Camden, who would have known him personally, described him as 'a most sharp maintainer of the purer religion', and he undoubtedly believed that in his labours he was battling against anti-Christ and all his works.

High on the list of these works Walsingham numbered 'the bosom serpent', Mary Queen of Scots. 'So long as that devilish woman lives', he had written to the Earl of Leicester in January 1572, 'neither her Majesty must make account to continue in quiet possession of her crown, nor her faithful servants assure themselves of safety of their lives.' As Secretary of State, Walsingham now found himself charged with overall responsibility for Mary, her welfare and her safekeeping. The Queen of Scots was still living under the guardianship of the Earl of Shrewsbury, but Shrewsbury took his orders from Walsingham and Walsingham's frankly stated mission in life was to frustrate the evil designs of Mary and her friends. Mary, of course, knew this and was for ever searching for ways and means of keeping open channels of communication with the outside world which would evade Walsingham's unsleeping watchfulness.

The Queen of Scots remained – officially – the Queen of England's 'guest', held in protective detention for her own good until such time as a way could be found to clear her name of the slur of murderess and honourably to restore her to her throne. But although Elizabeth continued from time to time to appear to seek a negotiated settlement to the problem, few informed observers of the political scene believed that Mary would ever return to Scotland. Meanwhile, Protestant England had to continue to shelter the papist snake in the grass in circumstances which, in the opinion of Francis Walsingham and those who shared his views on the Queen of Scots, were far too free and easy for comfort.

During the 1570s, when, significantly, the international situation was rather less menacing, the conditions of her captivity had become progressively more relaxed, and, not long after taking up his new post, Walsingham began to suspect that she was once more contriving to smuggle letters past the Earl of Shrewsbury's regrettably lax security system. In the spring of 1574 a Scottish stable-lad named Steward confessed to having delivered letters from Mary to her friends north of the border. According to Steward, these letters had been passed to him by another Scot, one Alexander Hamilton, employed as a tutor in the Shrewsbury household. But as Hamilton flatly denied any knowledge of Steward or having any dealings with the Scottish Queen, and as Steward refused to come to England to repeat his accusations, no charges could be brought. Walsingham, though, went on worrying away at the problem and at last, in January of the following year, further information coming from Scotland enabled him to proceed with the arrest of Henry Cockyn, stationer and bookseller of the city of London.

At first Cockyn proved uncommunicative, but in the Tower and subjected to the time-honoured technique of alternate bribery – if he would tell all he knew 'both he and his should be the better for it, and besides that the matter should be handled with such secrecy as he should not be discovered to be an accuser of others' – and threat – 'by torture he should be made to confess the bottom of the matter' – the bookseller became more persuadable and was finally induced to make a statement. This revealed that for the past year the enterprising Master Cockyn's shop had been used as a post office for the Queen of Scots' incoming and outgoing mail. Several of Shrewsbury's servants, including Alexander Hamilton, were implicated, as was Thomas Morgan, a one-time secretary to the Earl of Shrewsbury, who had shown up on the edges of the Ridolfi affair, when he had been mentioned as being 'a great intelligencer' of the Bishop of Ross, and who had since been suspected of further involvement in the Queen of Scots' intrigues. These were the couriers. More serious was Cockyn's disclosure that the correspondents had included Lord Henry Howard, brother of the late Duke of Norfolk, and the Duke's son, Philip.

With memories of the Ridolfi plot still so fresh, finding the existence of even the most superficial contact persisting between the Howard family and Mary Stewart was enough to set alarm bells ringing in government circles. But Elizabeth refused to take the matter too seriously. There was a spate of arrests among the couriers and the Howards were spoken to, but when it appeared they had done nothing more indiscreet than exchange friendly greetings with the Scottish Queen, the English Queen was easily persuaded 'that the matters they are charged withal are of no great consequence.' It happened that just at that moment Elizabeth was anxious to do nothing which might unnecessarily disturb the Anglo-French *entente*. Charles IX had died the previous spring at the age of twenty-four – the judgement of God, said the Protestants, but more likely from the effects of the congenital syphilis which riddled the French royal family – and the new King, his brother, was believed to incline towards the ultra Catholic faction of Mary Stewart's Guise relations.

So, after a few months detention the eleven men accused by Henry Cockyn were quietly released – with the exception, that is, of Thomas Morgan, who, forewarned of his impending arrest, had slipped over to France with the connivance, some said, of the English authorities.

Francis Walsingham was not best pleased with the outcome of the Cockyn episode, feeling that much of his hard work had been wasted and that the Queen's lack of concern would have the effect of discouraging 'all honest ministers that are careful for her safety to deal in the discovery of the sores of this diseased state.' He had, however, succeeded, at least temporarily, in closing down the Queen of Scots' private postal service and had been given a useful insight into the way Elizabeth's mind worked – how her attitude towards Mary and her own reactionary, crypto-Catholic nobility would always be governed by considerations of political pragmatism rather than those of Protestant religious purity. The case of Henry Cockyn had also confirmed all of Walsingham's misgivings about the suitability and efficiency of the Shrewsburys in their capacity as custodians of the bosom serpent.

By the mid-1570s the lull which had followed the trial and execution of the Duke of Norfolk was over, and from then until the end of the reign the history of the English secret service was one of continually tracking the progress of a stream of conspiracies, home grown and foreign or both, which varied widely in feasibility but all had as their prime objective the overthrow of the Protestant state, the removal of Queen Elizabeth and her replacement by the Queen of Scots.

In 1576/7 an ingenious plan for an invasion of England was being canvassed by the King of Spain's bastard half-brother, the colourful and popular warrior Don John of Austria, recently appointed Governor General of the Netherlands. The idea was that Don John should mount his attack under cover of an evacuation of the Spanish army in the Low Countries, having first concluded a peace settlement with the Dutch rebels. In December 1576 Don John proposed to inform the Queen of England of his intention to send his troops home by sea, at the same time requesting permission for them to take shelter in her ports should they be driven upon the English coast by storms! This, reported Thomas Wilson, Elizabeth's agent in the Low Countries, was believed to be 'a cloak for another matter', and Walsingham was soon receiving information about Don John's real intentions from a variety of sources. These included Amyas Paulet, his successor at the Paris embassy, who had heard from the Duke of Guise's secretary that a marriage was being arranged between Don John and the Queen of Scots. William of Orange himself had also heard rumours of a marriage between Mary Stewart and Don John together with a plot to poison Elizabeth, and passed on a warning early in February 1577. Spies among the English Catholic expatriate community in Flanders added that word was that negotiations were in progress with Don John for Mary's release, and full details of the affair were finally brought to light when a packet of Don John's letters were intercepted by the Huguenot commander François de la Noue. La Noue sent these letters to William of Orange, who had them deciphered and showed them to Dr Daniel Rogers, another English diplomat currently on a mission to the Dutch leader. Thus the eyes and ears of Protestant Europe combined to frustrate Catholic treachery but, in fact, the danger in this case had never been very great since Don John never managed to make peace with the implacably suspicious Dutch – an essential prerequisite to any invasion of England. The English government was, nevertheless, relieved when the victor of Lepanto died of plague in the autumn of 1578.

Francis Walsingham had experienced few problems in keeping abreast of Don John of Austria's designs via the normal official and semi-official channels of communication, nor did he have much difficulty in monitoring the activities of another equally picturesque individual who was at large in Europe at this time. Thomas Stukeley, or Stewkeley, originally of Ilfracombe in Devon, had, in the course of a varied career, been a mercenary soldier of fortune, a pirate, treasure hunter, company promoter, confidence trickster and rogue. At the beginning of the 1570s he was to be found in Ireland, involved, as usual, in some dubious financial transaction. Summoned back to London but feeling it might be unwise to obey, Stukeley sailed instead for Spain to offer his sword and his services to the Catholic cause. He got a warm welcome and a pension from Philip, served under Don John in his campaign against the Turks and fought bravely at the battle of Lepanto. He subsequently turned up in Rome, where he succeeded in conning the Vatican – in particular, the influential papal secretary Cardinal Como – into listening to a harebrained scheme for mounting an invasion of Ireland which would harass and exhaust 'that wicked woman' Elizabeth of England just as the Dutch rebels were harassing and exhausting Philip of Spain. Eventually, in January 1578, Stukeley did actually sail from the Italian port of Ostia with one leaky, illcaulked, ill-furnished ship. He got as far as Lisbon, where the King of Portugal persuaded him to abandon the Irish project and join a Portuguese expedition against the Moors instead. This proved an unfortunate decision for Stukeley, as a cannonball at Alcazar presently removed him permanently from the scene.

Walsingham had known about Stukeley's plans for at least a year from Henry Gilpin, an English merchant trading in Naples, and from an anonymous informant in Rome itself reporting to Christopher Hoddesdon, an agent of the Muscovy Company based in Hamburg. Thomas Wilson in the Low Countries was also on the watch and in June, Amyas Paulet in Paris heard from an Irish friar newly arrived from Spain that Stukeley had reached Lisbon. The Privy Council took the matter seriously enough to muster a force of two thousand men ready to send to Ireland if need be, and Henry Sydney, the Lord Deputy, was warned to keep a vigilant eye open for intruders until news that Stukeley's energies had been diverted towards Africa brought a general relaxation of tension.

It was, however, only a brief respite. Ireland, a soggy, impenetrable wilderness, where the tribes were controlled only with difficulty by the colonial government in Dublin, was the Elizabethan North-West Frontier, representing an expensive, ongoing and apparently insoluble problem to the Council in London and a well-nigh irresistible temptation to the Queen's enemies. Rome in particular continued to entertain great hopes of the Irish, and in 1579 James Fitzmaurice, a kinsman of the Earl of Desmond, together with the English Catholic activist Nicholas Sander and a handful of followers did actually make a landing in Dingle Bay on shores of Munster. They managed to raise the Desmonds but Fitzmaurice was killed quite early on, and although Sander kept the flame of rebellion alive for a time, the English had no particular difficulty in dealing with it.

The authorities had been expecting trouble, for yet again Walsingham had received ample advance warning of Fitzmaurice's plans and preparations – warning which had come in through the usual diplomatic channels, but principally from the Paris embassy, where Amyas Paulet was indefatigably collecting and collating reports from his network of Huguenot contacts. Walsingham's instinct, though, told him that Fitzmaurice's failure would not be the end of the affair. He felt convinced that help would come from Spain, and early in 1580 he arranged to receive special bulletins from selected English merchants trading on the Iberian coast – Roger Bodenham from San Lucar in the south, Botolphe Holder in Lisbon and John Dunne from Corunna and Santander. All three sent details of great naval preparations, most of which were undoubtedly connected with Philip's campaign against the Portuguese, but Dunne in the north picked up a story from a Spanish monk of forces being raised for Ireland.

Walsingham was also looking for information in France, where one of his agents, a man named Best, had succeeded in gaining the confidence of a secretary at the Spanish embassy, posing as an English defector in the hope of hearing something about the Irish threat. But it seems that Best's cover was blown, for he was killed in suspicious circumstances in a Paris street brawl that May. Walsingham had another plan to kidnap and interrogate the new papal legate on his way to France, using the Huguenot pirates operating out of La Rochelle as his hit men, but, perhaps fortunately, this remarkable project came to nothing.

The Queen was, as usual, hard to impress with a sense of her own danger, but she did agree to send reinforcements to Ireland and dispatched a squadron of four royal ships under Sir William Winter to patrol the Irish coast. In the event, the great naval preparations somewhat excitably overestimated as a fleet forty or sixty strong, turned into a couple of ships carrying about six hundred soldiers and volunteers who landed at Smerwick in September 1580 and were slaughtered almost to a man. After this latest debacle, even the cautious Walsingham felt that he could, for the time being at any rate, take Ireland off his list of most pressing problems. There were plenty of others to replace it, not least among them the arrival in the summer of 1580 of the first Jesuit missionary priests to set foot on English soil.

The missionary problem was not a new one. As long ago as 1568, the same year which had seen the flight of the Queen of Scots across the Solway Firth, a certain Dr William Allen, one-time Fellow of Oriel College Oxford, had rented a modest house in the university quarter of Douai, where a handful of English theological students could live and study under his direction. Allen, of Rossall in Lancashire, was one of that small but prestigious band of Englishmen unable to come to terms with the Elizabethan religious settlement. A fine scholar and possessing all the attributes of breeding, good looks and personal charm, he had thrown up a promising academic career to join the exile community in the Low Countries, but, unlike many of his compatriots, Allen could not be content simply to lament from a safe distance the collapse of Catholicism in England. Only too well aware that once the last of the old generation of pre-Reformation priests had died off 'no seed would be left hereafter for the restoration of religion, and that heresy would thus obtain a perpetual and peaceful possession of the realm', William Allen determined to take steps to prevent such a catastrophe. Towards the end of the 1560s, therefore, he was ready to set up a centre for exiled scholars where the flame of resistance could be kept alight and from which it might one day be possible to send missionaries suitably equipped to rally the old faithful and instruct the untaught young.

Allen was a born schoolmaster with the gift of being able to inspire real personal affection without loss of authority, and it was due in very large measure to the force of his personality and his unremitting hard work that the English College at Douai grew and flourished. As its fame spread a steady stream of students and visitors began to flow through its ever-open doors, and six years after its foundation the first contingent of Douai priests was ready to leave to gather 'the English harvest'. More soon followed, and by the end of the 1570s about a hundred missionaries had crossed the Channel, where, at least according to their own accounts, their success was immediate and spectacular. 'The number of Catholics increases so abundantly on all sides', wrote one of the pioneers to William Allen in 1575, 'that he who almost alone holds the rudder of the state [this was presumably Lord Burghley] has privately admitted to one of his friends that for one staunch Catholic at the beginning of the reign there were now, he knew for certain, ten.' Two years later Allen heard from people coming over to France that 'the numbers of those who were daily restored to the Catholic Church almost surpassed belief' and that 'one of the younger priests lately sent on the mission had reconciled no fewer than eighty persons in one day.'

Some allowance has to be made for wishful thinking in these reports and it also has to be remembered that the missionaries were to some extent preaching to the converted, in the sense that they naturally gravitated to Catholic houses and Catholic neighbourhoods finding shelter among sympathizers. But these young men were a very different breed of priest from the ignorant 'massmonger' of former times – the 'popish Sir John Mumblemattins' who all too often had done little more than gabble his unintelligible Latin prayers over a largely uncomprehending and indifferent congregation. The Douai priests, products of three years' intensive training and burning with the thirst for souls, were both willing and able to answer awkward questions, to discuss and resolve problems of conscience and expound points of doctrine. Most important of all, they were manifestly prepared to practise what they preached, to acept hardship and death 'for the deliverance of the Church and their brethren'. They came too late and too few to reverse the Protestant tide, but they did succeed in breathing new life into the dying embers of English Catholicism and keeping the flame alive.

The Catholic propaganda machine from its base in Belgium and indeed the missionaries themselves always maintained that the priests from Douai (and later from other European seminaries) were concerned only with pastoral matters, bringing the consolations of religion to those who wished for them. They were not interested in politics and had had nothing to do with procuring the Queen's excommunication, neither had they at any time any connection with 'any attempt against the realm or the prince's person'.

The Protestant establishment, both irritated and alarmed by the missionaries' activities, was not surprisingly unconvinced by these protestations. In the eyes of the Privy Council the Douai priests were subversives – Englishmen born who had chosen to transfer their allegiance to the Queen's avowed enemies. Were they not infiltrating the realm in disguise, using their religious proselytizing as a cover for their real purpose, which was to sow sedition, win subjects from their allegiance and encourage them to break the law, and also to practise conspiracies 'for the procurement and maintenance of the rebellion and wars against her Majesty and her realm'? To those who objected that the priests had come unarmed, as simple scholars and schoolmasters, Lord Burghley, in *The Execution of Justice*, a pamphlet setting out the official attitude to the missionaries, had this to say:

> Shall no subject that is a spial and explorer for the rebel or enemy against his natural prince be taken and punished as a traitor because he is not found with armour or weapon, but yet is taken in his disguised apparel, with scrolls and writings, or other manifest tokens, to prove him a spy for traitors, after he hath wandered secretly in his sovereign's camp, region, court or city?

And if anyone maintained that 'none are traitors that are not armed', then 'they will make Judas no traitor that came to Christ without armour, colouring his treason with a kiss.' The old argument as to whether the English Catholics and the missionary priests were being persecuted for their religion, or pursued as ordinary law-breakers and traitors is based on the false premiss that sixteenth-century religion and politics could be treated as separate issues. If that had ever been possible in Elizabethan England, *Regnans in Excelsis* and papal aggression in Ireland had effectively destroyed any chance that it might become possible again.

Although the government took a tough line with the priests from the beginning, in the earliest days the zeal with which they were hunted down depended to a large extent on the attitude of the local authorities. It was the arrival of the Jesuits or, to be precise, the arrival of the first batch of missionaries to include Jesuit fathers in their number, which raised the matter of the English mission to the status of a threat to national security. The Society or Company of Jesus had started life in 1534 as a small group of priests dedicated to practical social work among the poor, the heathen and the illiterate. Their founder, the crippled Spanish ex-soldier turned soldier of Christ, also dreamed of restoring the Catholic Church to the place of pre-eminence it had occupied in the Middle Ages. Ignatius Loyola believed passionately in the military virtues of discipline, efficiency and obedience, and while his ultimate aim may have been to put the clock back, he was not afraid to use modern methods, to adapt the old monastic ideal to meet the needs of the times. Loyola's new society was in no sense enclosed – in fact, he dispensed altogether with the normal obligation of a religious order to recite the office in choir. The Society of Jesus was to provide front-line troops for the Church, and therefore its members must be free at all times to go about in the world fighting the Church's battles wherever they were to be found. Loyola had passed through a phase of intense religious asceticism, but he was to prove himself a born leader, and when he died in 1556 his army had grown into a highly trained, well-organized body of men over a thousand strong.

Jesuit missionaries had followed the Conquistadores to America and penetrated as far as China and Japan in the east. Jesuit schools were already deservedly famous. Jesuit fathers held key positions in the Catholic universities of Europe and on the councils of many European rulers; they kept representatives at the Imperial Diet in

Germany; they were said to have the ear of Philip of Spain and to be whispering advice to Catherine de Medici in Paris. It was as palace politicians that the Jesuits made enemies, both inside and outside the Church, but it was on their proficiency as schoolmasters that their real power and influence rested. From teaching the children of the illiterate poor, they had progressed to teaching the children of the aristocracy – to the all-important task of forming the minds of each new generation of the international Catholic establishment – and in the spring of 1579 they had, at the request of William Allen himself, agreed to take over responsibility for running the recently founded English College in Rome. As an intellectual elite, the Society of Jesus was naturally attracting some of the best minds among the young men seeking ordination, as well as some of the most fervent souls. William Allen had seen a number of his own pupils join the Society, and while he would not stand in their way, he was saddened by the knowledge that a recruit won by the Jesuits had previously meant a labourer lost to the English harvest. Now it seemed this need no longer be the case, for that summer the General of the Jesuits was finally persuaded to allow some of his religious to enter the English mission field.

If the image of the Jesuit priest flitting through the corridors of power aroused complicated emotions of suspicion and jealousy among the members of longer established, less enterprising religious orders, the feelings it evoked in Protestant circles were not in the least complicated. To the English government, perennially (some would say morbidly) preoccupied with the dangers of subversion from within and encirclement and invasion from without, the Society of Jesus embodied everything they feared and hated most about Roman Catholicism. By the early 1580s the bogeyman of the 'pollyticke' Jesuit had become forever fixed in the official mind as the chief public enemy of the Protestant state, and official reaction to the news that Jesuit priests were actually planning to set their cloven hooves on Protestant soil was therefore excitable.

In fact, the superiors of the Order had been reluctant to involve themselves in the English harvest. The Jesuit General and his advisers knew that under present conditions in England it would be virtually impossible to keep the rules and discipline of the Society and they hesitated to send their members into such spiritual outer darkness. Apart from this, England was a political minefield which would need the most careful navigation if the missionaries were not to lay themselves open to charges of plotting and intrigue – thus damaging both the Society and the cause it served.

However, having once committed themselves, the Jesuits began preparing for the task ahead with their usual efficiency. Detailed instructions were drawn up for the guidance of the pioneers, who were to behave so that all might see 'that the one gain they covet is that of souls.' They were also to be very careful about the company they kept, for it was emphasized that the aim of the mission was 'the preservation and augmentation of the Faith of the Catholics of England', and the fathers were to avoid any temptation to dispute with heretics. In fact, they were to avoid contact with heretics altogether. Most important of all, 'they must not entangle themselves in affairs of State' or write to Rome about political matters. They were not to speak against the Queen, or allow others to do so in their presence, 'except perhaps in the company of those whose fidelity has been long and steadfast and even then not without strong reasons.' In a later version of the Instructions this proviso was omitted and the official prohibition on talking politics became absolute.

There was another matter which the Jesuits wanted settled: the debatable question of the continued force of *Regnans in Excelsis*. Were pious Catholics in England really obliged to consider themselves under interdict if they recognized and obeyed (in civil matters, at least) their deposed and schismatic Queen? During the ten years which had passed since Pius V had loosed the papal thunderbolts, none of William Allen's protégés had apparently thought it necessary to seek a ruling on this point. In typically English fashion, the problem had been quietly swept under the carpet and left there. This did not, however, satisfy the logical Latin minds which ruled the Society of Jesus, and they extracted an *Explanatio* from the current Pope, laying down that, although the provisions of the bull still applied in full to Queen Elizabeth and her herectical supporters, it in no way bound the English Catholics, 'except when public execution of the said bull shall become possible.' In other words, it seemed that the Queen's Catholic subjects might continue to accept her as their *de facto* sovereign until such time as means could be found to overthrow her. The Jesuits might have been wiser to have left well alone, for when, in due course, this interesting piece of information found its way into the hands of the English government, they showed no signs of gratitude for the respite thus thoughtfully provided.

In April 1580 a letter written from Rome to a friend of William Allen's, then at Rheims, was intercepted and forwarded to Francis Walsingham. It gave the news that a large party of Englishmen, including two Jesuit priests, Fathers Campion and Parsons, and a lay-brother, Ralph Emerson, had just left the Holy City for 'the English harvest'. The dispatch of Campion and Parsons marked the beginning of a new phase of Catholic missionary endeavour in England, but the impact made by the so-called 'Jesuit Invasion' of 1580 was due in large part to the exceptional qualities possessed by its two pioneers.

Edmund Campion was a Londoner, son of a bookseller who had been sponsored to grammar school and St John's College Oxford by one of the city livery companies. A brilliant scholar and, like William Allen, a born teacher, Campion soon made a name for himself as a tutor and lecturer. He was appointed proctor and public orator, his eloquence attracting special notice during the royal visit to Oxford in 1566, when the Queen recommended him to the patronage of the Earl of Leicester, Chancellor of the University, and Lord Burghley (or William Cecil, as he then was) also made a favourable note of the promising young Fellow of St John's. At the age of twenty-six, therefore, Edmund Campion had the world at his feet but, sadly, his conscience was beginning to stir. Like William Allen, he made the hard decision to turn his back on the glittering prizes and by the end of the 1560s had gone out into the cold of religious exile.

In addition to his persuasive intellectual gifts, Edmund Campion was blessed with the sort of sweetness of nature which disarms jealousy. Robert Parsons, by contrast, 'a man wonderfully given to scoffing', was renowned for his bitter, sarcastic tongue and a quite unusual talent for making enemies. A West Countryman, born in 1546 in the village of Nether Stowey on the edge of the Quantock Hills, said to be the son of a blacksmith, Parsons (or Persons) received a grammar-school education thanks to the encouragement of the vicar of his parish. He later went up to Oxford, studying logic at St Mary's Hall and becoming a Fellow of Balliol in 1568. Like Campion, he was a successful tutor, but his career at the university ended under a cloud, and in 1573 he was expelled from Balliol 'even with public ringing of bells'. Parsons himself claimed that he had been the victim of a conspiracy and the most likely explanation

67

seems to be that he had made himself so unpopular that his fellow dons had combined to get rid of him. In company with many of the younger Oxford men of his time, Robert Parsons had already begun to flirt with Catholicism, and two years after his ignominious exit from Balliol he was in Rome applying for admission to the Jesuit novitiate. The Society of Jesus seems to have been quick to recognize his executive, as well as his intellectual, abilities. He was an obvious candidate when it came to choosing the trail-blazers for the English mission and, although junior to Campion in both age and religion, Parsons was put in charge of the party.

It was obviously going to be no easy matter to get into England undetected and, after consulting with the leaders of the English community in St Omer, it was decided that Parsons should go ahead by the short sea-route to Dover, 'under the habit and profession of a captain returned from the Low Countries'. If all went well, Campion would follow, disguised as a merchant in precious stones, with Ralph Emerson as his servant. Although there was no official expeditionary force in the Netherlands as yet, quite a number of the Queen's subjects – some from conviction, but probably more out of a taste for rough games – were fighting with the Dutch rebels on a free-lance basis. The mercenary captain on his way to or from the wars was therefore a familiar enough sight at the Channel ports.

Parsons donned his new identity and military coat of buff leather with enthusiasm, arriving at Dover some time after midnight on 16 June without incident. Nor did he encounter any problems with the port authorities. No one, it seemed, saw any reason to suspect the dark, rugged-featured swaggering soldier, and Parsons was quick to follow up his advantage. He asked a friendly official to look out for his friend Mr Edmunds, and left a letter to be forwarded to St Omer, telling Campion that if he made haste, he could help him to sell his jewels.

Parsons then went on his way to London, and it was there, in the heart of enemy territory, that his troubles began. Innkeepers were suspicious of lone travellers on foot, and his military appearance, which had caused no surprise at the seaports, was uncomfortably conspicuous in the capital. Aware of curious glances being cast in his direction, Parsons realized that he was courting disaster by staying on the streets and, after walking up and down for half the day, 'resolved to adventure into the prison of the Marshalsea.' This was not quite such a desperate step as it sounds – though it provides an illuminating comment on the Elizabethan prison system. In general the 'better sort' of Catholics in gaol for simple recusancy were able to live in reasonable comfort – as long, that is, as they could pay for their comforts – and the Marshalsea was a five-star gaol, where the wealthier inmates could receive visitors, send messages and sometimes even get out for a while. Parsons felt confident of finding a friend somewhere inside, and he was not disappointed. Warmly welcomed, given dinner, introduced to some useful contacts and, before the day was over, borne off to a 'safe house' in the city, he could begin to relax a little. Ten days later Father Campion and Ralph Emerson had joined him, and soon the Jesuit mission was making waves. The newly arrived Spanish ambassador, Bernardino de Mendoza, reported in July that all those Catholics who had been released on bail were being ordered to surrender themselves within twenty days under pain of death.

Mendoza went on to state with rather more than pardonable exaggeration that the English Catholics were suffering greater travail and persecution than they had ever been afflicted with before, but it was true that the years of tacit toleration accorded to the peaceable Catholic minority were coming to an end. An official proclamation just issued restating the Queen's determination to retain her people in 'the true profession of the Gospel and free from the bondage of Roman tyranny', also warned any who harboured 'unnatural affections' not to irritate Her Majesty into using the rod or sword of justice against them. Plans were being drawn up for the stricter segregation of Catholic prisoners, especially 'the principal persons of most mark', and preparatory steps taken towards the strengthening of the anti-recusancy laws. In the autumn of 1580, however, the Queen's government was concentrating its efforts on the most effective counter-measure of all – that of catching the missionary priests, and especially the Jesuits Campion and Parsons, both of whom were now on tour round the southern counties, preaching and administering the sacraments in every gentleman's or nobleman's house they passed where any Catholics were to be found.

Robert Parsons has left a vivid description of what it felt like to be part of such a household when a priest was being entertained. He wrote,

> Sometimes, when we are sitting at table quite cheerfully, conversing familiarly about matters of faith or piety (for this is the most frequent subject of conversation), it happens that someone

knocks on the front door a little more insistently than usual, so that he can be put down as an official. Immediately, like deer that have heard the huntsman and prick up their ears, all stand to attention, stop eating and commend themselves to God in the briefest of prayers. No word or sound of any sort is heard until the servants come to report what the matter is. If it turns out that there is no danger, we laugh at our fright.

Many Catholic families had already taken the precaution of providing secret places where a wanted man could be hidden in case of emergency. As time went on, the construction of such hides, or priest's holes, became a highly skilled and specialized craft – Nicholas Owen, son of an Oxford carpenter, being its most noted practitioner. But in the early days, the hiding places were often amateurish affairs and known to too many people, so that the priests would prefer to take refuge in woods and thickets, lying in ditches or even holes in the ground. The atmosphere, Parsons noted, was reminiscent of the primitive church. Mass was celebrated in attics and cellars, in barns and caves and, not surprisingly in such circumstances, the emotional temperature was high.

After about two-and-a-half months on the road, Parsons sent Campion up to Lancashire for the winter and himself returned to London. He was fully aware of the risk he was running and told a friend in Rome that although he had many places in the capital where he could stay, 'yet in none of them do I remain beyond two days, owing to the extremely careful searches that have been made to capture me.' On at least two occasions he evaded the net spread for him by the narrowest of margins. In November a group of Catholic gentlemen were arrested when the Red Rose public house in Holborn was raided. Parsons was expected at this gathering and was actually on his way there, but although he knew the district well, he failed to find the rendezvous – possibly because he enquired for it by its other name, the Red Lion. Next day he heard that the door had been shut and 'the secretary Walsingham's men within it that were sent to apprehend me.' Not long afterwards he was visiting a house in Tothill Fields when the searchers arrived, and he only escaped 'by running into the haymow'.

In spite of the strain imposed by the necessity of being constantly one step ahead of the government's bloodhounds and constantly on the move, Parsons from his base in the capital had virtually taken over control of the mission's operations. As well as celebrating

Mass and preaching, sometimes twice in one day, struggling with 'almost unending business', solving problems of conscience, organizing the activities of the other missionaries, reconciling schismatics, encouraging the faint-hearted, chivvying backsliders and trying to arrange help for those in prison and in want, he was thinking of the future. He nagged the authorities in Rome for reinforcements – a supply of 'numerous soldiers, courageous for the battle' – and he set up a network of lay helpers, or 'sub-seminaries' as they became known. These young men, all scions of well-to-do Catholic or crypto-Catholic families and all with plenty of spare time as well as spare cash to devote to the cause, acted as guides, couriers and bankers for the missionary priests. They performed an invaluable service and since the prospect of taking the field with the heroic fathers and sharing something of the danger and excitement of their work appealed strongly to idealistic youth, there was never any shortage of volunteers.

Although he admitted to feeling weary, the amazing Robert Parsons was to add yet another task to his already overwhelming work-load in that winter of 1580–1. In spite of all the government's effort to suppress it, book-running – the illegal importation of works of Catholic propaganda and devotion from the Continental presses – was still going on, and now Parsons conceived the bold idea of setting up his own underground press in or near London. The technical problems involved were formidable – a 'safe' place had to be found to house the press, printers and binders recruited and supplies of paper and type got together without arousing suspicion – but Parsons was not easily discouraged by technical difficulties and in due course the secret press was established at Greenstreet House, situated between the then outlying suburban villages of East Ham and Barking. Parsons himself wrote the first book to be printed – a *Brief Discourse* explaining why Catholics refused to attend the Church of England service – and in all some six books or pamphlets were produced and distributed under conditions of extreme difficulty. The best known of these was the *Decem Rationes*, a learned Latin treatise running to about 20,000 words composed by Edmund Campion during his sojourn in the comparatively secure Catholic north-west. Parsons felt that Campion ought to come south to superintend the printing of this important and complicated piece of polemic and the two Jesuits foregathered in the spring of 1581 at Stonor Park near Henley, where the press was now operating.

By this time the fathers had been at large for nearly a year and there is no doubt that their mission was having a strongly inspirational effect on the Catholic minority. In the words of a London preacher, who clearly believed in calling a spade a spade, 'the Papists and Jesuites, with other the riffe raffe and scumme of this Realme are nowe seen to appeare, who before this tyme have beene hidden in the dytches and channelles of England.' Official disquiet was reflected in the increased number of arrests and generally much harder line being taken against the Catholic laity, and also in the much stiffer anti-Catholic legislation passed by the 1581 Parliament. It now became a treasonable offence to attempt to persuade any of the Queen's subjects to leave the Church of England for the 'pretended authority of the See of Rome', and the penalties for saying or hearing Mass and refusing to attend the Protestant service had risen steeply.

At the beginning of July, Edmund Campion had finished his work of seeing the *Decem Rationes* through the press and was ready to take the road again, meaning to return to Lancashire to collect his books and other belongings before going on a tour of Norfolk. But first he was anxious to accept a long-standing and pressing invitation to visit Lyford Grange, a well-known Catholic household in Berkshire. Unhappily for Campion, someone else was planning to pay a visit to Lyford. George Elliot was not untypical of that class of person who had found in the laying of information a ready-made solution to their personal and financial problems. In its campaign against the missionary priests the government was obliged to rely heavily on informers and could not afford to be over-fussy about their characters or antecedents. Elliot is said to have been in prison facing a charge of murder when he got in touch with the Earl of Leicester offering his services, but he had at one time been a Catholic and had worked in various Catholic houses, both useful qualifications for a priest catcher, and he was therefore let out of gaol to begin a startlingly successful career as one of those 'false brethren' who constituted by far the greatest single danger to those working in the English mission field.

Whether or not it was mere chance that Elliot should have been in the neighbourhood of Lyford at the time of Campion's visit is uncertain, but the Grange was an obvious target for one of his profession and when he presented himself there on Sunday, 16 July, posing as a devout member of the faithful eager to hear Mass, he gained admission without difficulty; the cook, who had known him in the days when he had been steward to Mr Roper of Orpington, whispering that he would be lucky enough to hear Father Campion preach. Elliot just had time to send his companion, one David Jenkins, to find a magistrate, before proceeding decorously to the chapel, where a congregation of some sixty people was assembled. He sat through the Mass and Campion's sermon on the all too appropriate text 'Jerusalem, Jerusalem, thou that killest the prophets'. Elliot, Judas Elliot, as he was to become known, then hurriedly took his leave, refusing a pressing invitation to stay to dinner. This in itself should have aroused suspicion, but in the general euphoria of the moment no one seems to have noticed the stranger's abrupt departure – indeed the security arrangements seem to have been remarkably casual. Only one look-out had been posted, and while the company was still at the dinner table he came panting in with the horrifying information that the house was surrounded by armed men. Campion wanted to be allowed to take his chance outside. He might even now be able to slip through the cordon, but his hosts would not hear of such a thing and Campion and two other priests who were also present were hustled away into a secret place opening out of one of the upper rooms just as the first hammering fell on the front door.

To begin with, the search party, made up of local men dragged away from their normal Sunday pursuits, showed no great enthusiasm for the task in hand. They found nothing and were only too willing to call off the hunt. But Elliot was not going to be cheated of his triumph by a parcel of ignorant yokels. Did they really expect to find Campion, notorious Jesuit and traitor, hiding under a bed or keeping company with the rest of the family, he demanded scornfully and, flourishing his royal warrant, insisted on a more thorough search being made. The magistrate, much as he may have resented having to take orders from this jumped-up jack-in-office, had no choice but to obey. At their second attempt the search party uncovered several likely hiding places, but no priests. It was growing dark by this time and operations were suspended until the following day, Elliot and a select band of helpers remaining on guard.

Next morning it all began again – the examining of every cupboard, closet and chimney, tapping the wainscot for hollow sounds, hacking at suspicious plaster, tearing up the floorboards, but still nothing. Tension in the house mounted unbearably as it began to look as if the miracle was going to happen. Then, just as Elliot prepared sulkily to admit defeat, someone – was it perhaps Elliot himself? – glanced up and noticed a chink of light over the stairwell, in a place where no chink of light should have been. A section of wall was opened up with a crowbar, and there were the three priests in a space just large enough for them to lie side by side.

Campion was carried off to London to imprisonment, interrogation, torture, trial and a traitor's death, but Robert Parsons' phenomenal luck still held. Even when Stonor was raided and the secret press seized, Parsons had just left on a visit to Windsor. He retreated to Michelgrove in Sussex, where he was unexpectedly offered an opportunity to cross over to France with a party of Catholic refugees. It was a difficult decision to make, but Parsons was now on the run, and if he stayed in England his capture could only be a matter of weeks, perhaps days. Once across the Channel he would be able to make a detailed report to his superiors and discuss the needs of the mission with William Allen in person. Of the reinforcements he had begged from the Society of Jesus, Fathers Heywood and Holt had already arrived and should be able to carry on for a while. On the other hand, Parsons, who has been described as one of the most able, most interesting and most misunderstood men of his generation, knew that it would look as if he were deserting his post and worried about the possible effect on morale. But the issue was never really in doubt. Edmund Campion could serve the cause by dying nobly a martyr's death. Robert Parsons' vein of earthy, peasant common sense told him that he could serve it best by staying alive. He left England some time between 13 and 21 August and was to devote the rest of his life to working unceasingly for the hopeless dream of the Great Enterprise.

Although Parsons' escape would have been a matter of regret, Francis Walsingham could not but be relieved that he and Campion were no longer at large to trouble the Church of God in England. Nor is there any reason to doubt that he fully agreed with his brother-in-law Walter Mildmay, who had recently urged the need in the House of Commons for sterner measures to be taken against all 'obstinate and stiff-necked Papists', singling out 'a sort of hypocrites, naming themselves Jesuits', a rabble of vagrant friars sent in most underhand fashion by the Pope to creep into reputable men's houses 'not only to corrupt the realm with false doctrine, but also, under that pretence, to stir sedition.' Throughout his service Francis Walsingham was to be a vocal member of the lobby pressing for sterner measures to be taken against all purveyors of invasive papistry, but at the beginning of the 1580s he was looking apprehensively northward. For the first time since the flight of Mary Queen of Scots serious danger was threatening from the other side of the Border, danger the more alarming for being glimpsed only in snatches and which was to provide Walsingham's secret service with its first major challenge.

CHAPTER FOUR

The sacred enterprise

───────◆───────

From earliest times England's relations with her northern neighbour had been, if not actively hostile, at best in a state of uneasy truce, and the political score in Edinburgh thus remained a matter of vital concern in London. Since the last remnants of the Marian faction had been rooted out in the early 1570s, the pro-English party had held power unchallenged; but after nearly a decade of quite unusual calm, the situation was changing and several potentially destabilizing factors beginning to emerge. One of these was Mary Stewart's son, James, now in his early teens and about to step out on to the international stage. Another – more ominous – was the threatened re-awakening interest in Scottish affairs by Mary's French cousins. Young James might still be pretty much of an unknown quantity – the Guise family were not, and while any revival of the Franco-Scottish connection, the 'auld alliance' between her two nearest enemies, spelt bad news for England, the first hint of Guise involvement was enough to set alarm bells jangling in Whitehall. It was, after all, a well-known fact that the Guises, with their strong vested interest in promoting the cause of the Queen of Scots, never lost an opportunity of stirring up trouble for the Queen of England.

Such an opportunity arose in the summer of 1579, when a dispute concerning the estate of the Earl of Lennox, King James's paternal grandfather, brought Esme Stuart, the Seigneur d'Aubigny and a nephew of the late Earl, over from France. D'Aubigny travelled to Edinburgh at James's invitation, ostensibly to stake a claim to the Lennox patrimony but also carrying a secret commission from his friend and patron the Duke of Guise, who had asked him to try and win the confidence of the young King and revitalize the French party in Scotland. Not surprisingly, the young King, who had been raised according to strict Calvinistic principles, found the companionship of his good-looking, charming and accomplished kinsman an altogether delightful novelty. Within a matter of months d'Aubigny, or the Earl and then Duke of Lennox as he rapidly became, assisted by his henchman Captain James Stewart, had established their ascendancy at the Scottish Court. Before the end of 1580 they had engineered the overthrow of the government headed by the unlikeable but reliably pro-English Regent Morton, and by January 1581 the Spanish ambassador in London was reporting gleefully that the news from Scotland was that the King had quite changed his tone, 'd'Aubigny governing him entirely and the whole country'.

Bernardino de Mendoza was confidently expecting trouble from the Scots – 'they show great inclination to make war upon the English' – and so, despite the public assurances of friendship coming from Lennox, did Francis Walsingham. Walsingham knew all about Esme Stuart's Guisard connections and had also been told by his friend Paulet at the Paris embassy that before leaving France, d'Aubigny had had a long private meeting with the Queen of Scots' ambassador, the Archbishop of Glasgow. Not surprisingly, therefore, the Secretary of State feared that 'some great and hidden treason not yet discovered' was brewing behind England's always vulnerable back door. Urgent signals were sent out to Henry Cobham, Paulet's successor in Paris, and to Robert Bowes, English ambassador in Scotland, ordering them to make every effort to find out what d'Aubigny was up to; but although rumours proliferated – the Sieur d'Aubigny was said to be buying arms in the Low Countries, to be in frequent contact with the Duke of Guise, to have promised the Pope to leave nothing undone for the advancing of the Scottish Queen and Catholicism – hard information remained disquietingly difficult to come by. In August Walsingham was himself in Paris on a diplomatic mission and while there he heard, probably from his agent, Thomas Rogers, then operating undercover in Rome, about a plan for an invasion of Scotland which had been sent to the Pope the previous June and which apparently had gained the support of the King of Spain. Walsingham also heard from Henry Cobham that the Duke of Guise was busy advocating d'Aubigny's cause with the King of France and an intercepted letter from the Queen of Scots to the Archbishop of Glasgow revealed that Mary knew all about her cousin's 'designs', though unfortunately did not reveal what they were.

Walsingham's failure to pick up a scent on this occasion was pretty certainly due to the fact that Guisard and papal plans for exploiting the situation in Scotland were still barely formulated. This is not to say that a variety of such plans were not beginning to take shape. In October 1581 Robert Parsons, now established with his printing press at Rouen in northern France, wrote to the Jesuit General expressing his belief that 'the greatest hope we have lies in Scotland, on which country depends the conversion not only of England but of all the lands in the North.' Parsons had already dispatched an English priest, William Watts, to carry out a preliminary reconnaissance, and in September, by which time the initiative had passed to the Spanish embassy, Mendoza sent Watts back to Scotland with instructions 'to try to get a private interview with d'Aubigny, and tell him that, if the King would submit to the Roman Catholic Church, many of the English nobles and a great part of the population would at once side with him and have him declared heir to the English crown and release his mother.' Watts proceeded cautiously – he was not entirely sure of Lennox with his French connections and had his doubts as to the sincerity of the Scottish nobles. On his return to London towards the end of October he told Mendoza that he thought the best argument to bring about James's conversion – apart, of course, from its being the true road to salvation – would be to show him 'that it was the only means by which he could become a powerful King, uniting the crowns of Scotland, England and Ireland.'

Whether or not James would rise to the bait remained in doubt, but all through the winter of 1581-2 plans were being actively discussed for a Catholic *coup d'état* in Scotland to be followed by an invasion of England by way of the border. The threads of this elaborate conspiracy stretched from Bernardino de Mendoza at the Court of St James to Mary Queen of Scots in her prison at Sheffield Castle, from Lennox at Holyrood to the Duke of Guise, Robert Parsons, William Allen and the Spanish and papal representatives in France, while two Jesuit fathers, Holt and Creighton, commuted between London, Edinburgh and Paris carrying letters and messages, suggestions and promises. Progress at first was slow – there was a good deal of mutual distrust to be overcome, distances were considerable and the need for secrecy meant that no corners could be cut – but at last, in April 1582, Father Creighton arrived in Paris from Scotland with a letter for King Philip's ambassador, Juan Bautista de Tassis, from the Duke of Lennox.

Egged on by Creighton, Lennox had finally agreed to commit himself to the 'design' which, he was told, the Pope and the King of Spain had in hand for the restoration of the Catholic religion and the liberation of the Queen of Scotland – providing he was guaranteed adequate backing, and he had listed his requirements in a memorandum to be passed on by Creighton to the appropriate quarters. Lennox's ideas of what constituted adequate backing were optimistic: an army of 20,000 mercenaries paid for eighteen months, together with a number of pioneers, plenty of artillery and munitions plus the sum of 20,000 crowns. When de Tassis raised his eyebrows at the size of these demands, Creighton and Parsons hurriedly reassured him that, of course, Lennox would leave such matters to be settled by the Duke of Guise, who was of the opinion that a force of 6,000–8,000 troops would be ample. Guise himself was full of enthusiasm for the project and proposed making a diversionary landing on the coast of Sussex 'to put the whole kingdom into confusion.'

Robert Parsons went on to tell de Tassis that the English Catholics were eager for the design to be carried out, and that if arms were taken up in Scotland 'with a well grounded prospect of success', they would come flocking to join the invading army. The north, especially 'all that part which borders upon Scotland', was well known to be full of Catholics, and if the Pope would name some influential person for the great bishopric of Durham (Parsons had William Allen in mind) he would be able to raise the people. There were other persons who would do the same in other districts, for England was 'so full of Catholics that it could not be believed.'

Having just spent more than a year in England, Parsons could reasonably be accepted as a credible authority, but de Tassis was not entirely convinced. He wrote to Philip:

> When I asked him what security they have for all this, and whether any of the principal men had formed a confederation for this object and given each other some security of signatures, as the custom is, he [Parsons] answered me that he knew all this from what many of them had declared when he had treated with them of their consciences.

If the ambassador thought this an evasion of the issue, he was careful not to say so and, having received no briefing from Madrid, listened to his visitors 'with a friendly countenance', trying 'neither to divert them in any way from what they propose, nor yet to give them encouragement.'

The two Jesuits spent the next six weeks putting the final touches to their 'design'. Several conferences were held with the Duke of Guise, William Allen, the Archbishop of Glasgow, the papal nuncio and the sceptical de Tassis to discuss points of detail; although snags such as the fact that the army to be landed in Scotland, whether 6,000 or 20,000 strong, existed only on paper; that the Duke of Guise, despite his soubriquet of King of Paris, was not King of France, and that Henri III, poor creature though he might be, would certainly warn Queen Elizabeth of any Guisard plot against her the moment he heard about it, were brushed aside. But not even the most invincibly optimistic of the conspirators could ignore the fact that no action of any kind would take place until the Pope and the King of Spain had been persuaded to part with something more substantial than moral support. Accordingly, at the end of May, Father Creighton set off for Rome and Robert Parsons for Lisbon, where Philip was then in residence.

Soon after this, Francis Walsingham's intelligence service had a small stroke of luck, when one of Mendoza's couriers – probably the priest William Watts – was intercepted near the Scottish border by a patrol operating under the command of Sir John Forster, Warden of the Middle Marches. The courier, who was travelling disguised as an itinerant tooth-drawer, managed to bribe his way out of trouble, but he left behind a looking-glass which Mendoza had had specially made with a false back for the concealment of private correspondence. When this unusual piece of dental equipment was delivered to Sir John Forster, he found it to contain letters addressed to the Duke of Lennox, which he promptly passed on to Francis Walsingham. Unfortunately from Walsingham's point of view, Mendoza had written only in 'general terms', but there was enough in the captured documents to provide confirmation of the existence of a conspiracy involving all Protestant England's principal dreads – the Queen of Scots, the King of Spain, the Duke of Guise and the Jesuits.

But although Walsingham received a report from Berwick in July that Lennox 'bears all the sway with the King [James], and what he will have him to do, it is done', there were also indications that his reign might be coming to an end. 'The whole nobility – at least the best part – are grievously offended with the government of the Duke of Lennox', wrote the Earl of Angus, and 'the ministers in their sermons daily cry out against the proceedings of the Duke of Lennox.'

Discreetly prodded from London, the Kirk and the Protestant lords had now decided that Lennox and his Catholic friends had had a long enough run. On 22 August, therefore, the Earls of Angus, Gowrie and Mar kidnapped King James in the so-called Raid of Ruthven. Lennox, who had received advance warning of their intentions, fled to Dumbarton Castle, where he took refuge for a while but was presently obliged ignominiously to apply to Queen Elizabeth for a safe-conduct to return to France by way of England. The Duke was out of the game and by the following spring he was dead 'of a sickness contracted through displeasure'.

The Raid of Ruthven came as a bad blow to the Franco-Spanish conspirators, but they were not discouraged for long. When the first news reached Paris, de Tassis told King Philip that Hercules (code name of the Duke of Guise) was certainly distressed but still eager to undertake the enterprise. By the following spring, however, Hercules, 'seeing matters in Scotland altered, and with but small probability of promptly assuming a position favourable for the plans that had been formed, has now turned his eyes towards the English Catholics, to see whether the affair might not be commenced there.' Throughout the summer of 1583, therefore, plans for a reconstructed 'holy enterprise' were being worked out. Although James had regained his freedom of action in June, Parsons and Allen both advised that, while the state of Scotland and the King's religious intentions remained so uncertain, a direct invasion of England offered the best chance of success. A Spanish force of about 5,000 men, drawn from the Duke of Parma's army in the Netherlands, commanded by the Duke of Guise and accompanied by all the English exiles, was to land at the Pile of Fouldrey on the Lancashire coast, where it would be joined by a further force of 20,000 native Catholics. It would then proceed to liberate Mary Stewart and dispose of Elizabeth in an unspecified but, it must be assumed, permanent fashion – 'rendering her impotent to injure or offend' was how Mendoza put it.

In September, Charles Paget, an English dissident who had gone into exile in France a couple of years earlier and who was to become closely involved with the Queen of Scots, crossed the Channel on a secret mission for the Duke of Guise. Paget's instructions were to confer with the Catholic gentry of Sussex and Surrey and try to enlist their support for the invasion plan. He was to assure them, 'on the faith and honour of Hercules', that the enterprise was being undertaken with no other object than to re-establish the Catholic religion in England, 'and to place the Queen of Scotland peacefully on the throne of England, which rightly belongs to her.' Once this had been achieved, the foreigners would, of course, immediately withdraw.

Strong efforts were also being made to persuade the Pope 'that now was the time for acting, that there had never been a like opportunity, nor would such a chance ever recur.' The Holy Father, as always, lent a sympathetic ear, but could not be cajoled into authorizing the transfer of any papal gold – not, at least, until he was sure of the King of Spain – and the King of Spain, while continuing to pay lip service to the projected Guisard invasion of England, showed no signs of being willing to authorize the transfer of any Spanish troops from the Netherlands. In fact, he showed no sign of being prepared to offer any practical assistance to the conspirators and his correspondence with Mendoza in London reveals considerable private scepticism, rooted in his distrust of the French royal and ruling class.

This was a distrust shared by his ambassador. Apart from being unable to subdue the heretics in their own realm, wrote Mendoza in July, 'the French put the question of religion into a second place, as a mere accessory after politics, and in this even they are not steadfast, but are swayed by their appetite and interest for overbearing and insolent domination.' Nevertheless, Mendoza remained convinced that the interests of God and the King of Spain would best be served by the elevation of Mary Queen of Scots to the throne of a converted England and that the Duke of Guise should be given every possible help in his undertaking. As Mary's closest kinsman, he was the obvious man for the job and for both their sakes could be trusted to resist any French take-over bid. 'Guise also will have to look to your Majesty, who provides the expedition', wrote Mendoza. While, as for Mary, she would undoubtedly lean on Philip as her main support, knowing that he had rescued her from her former miserable state.

But Philip, although he could hardly say so publicly, placed no such reliance on the Scottish Queen's gratitude. When push came to shove, the King of Spain's reluctance to risk seeing England drawn into the French sphere of influence outweighed every other consideration, even that of the Catholic Church. In October he finally withdrew his support and the whole house of cards so laboriously constructed by Guise and his Jesuit allies collapsed in ruins.

Meanwhile, Francis Walsingham was still patiently pursuing his enquiries at the English end of the puzzle. In September 1582 the Scots had captured George Douglas – the same who had once organized Queen Mary's escape from Lochleven – and forced him (under torture, according to Mendoza) to confess details of a mission he had undertaken to France to confer with the Duke of Guise on the Duke of Lennox's behalf. Douglas also admitted that he and Lennox had been in regular communication with Mary via the Archbishop of Glasgow in Paris and the French ambassador in London.

The following spring a much bigger fish was landed when the Jesuit William Holt, betrayed by a renegade priest while he waited at Leith for a passage to France, fell into the hands of the Scottish authorities. At his preliminary interrogation Holt confessed that the Pope and certain Catholic princes did indeed have 'a purpose in hand' to make war on England in the cause of religion and for the advancement of the Queen of Scots. He added that the Pope was preparing to subsidize the said purpose and that the King of Spain was expected to play a leading part, but 'of the time, the instruments to be used and other particularities' he pretended, wrote one of the English agents in Edinburgh, to know nothing.

Greatly cheered by the news of Holt's capture, Walsingham at once sent instructions northwards that the prisoner should be 'substantially examined and forced by torture to deliver what he knoweth.' The Secretary of State was convinced that Holt had been used as a 'special instrument' by Mauvissière, the French ambassador in London, and by Lennox, and had no doubt but that he possessed vital information regarding the 'intended practices' against both England and Scotland. In fact, few knew more about these practices than Father Holt, but he was fortunate in having powerful friends among the Scottish Catholic nobility who, to Walsingham's intense irritation, persuaded King James to wink at

83

his escape from custody before anything useful could be extracted from him.

This was a serious disappointment, especially so since Walsingham had now reached the firm conclusion that the key to the whole business lay in France. In a sense, of course, he was quite right, although, rather surprisingly for one with his intimate knowledge of French affairs, he seems not to have taken account of the long-standing antipathy which existed between the Guises and the King of France. So, not realizing that the conspirators were going to a good deal of trouble to keep Henri III and his ambassador in ignorance of their intentions, Walsingham settled down to watch the French embassy like puss at a mousehole. In this he was helped by a recent recruit to his intelligence staff. William Fowler, a young Scot educated in France, speaking the language fluently and possessing some very useful family connections – his father had been friendly with the old Countess of Lennox, Mary Stewart's former mother-in-law, and had lent money to the Scottish Queen herself – was ideally suited to the task of gaining the confidence of the French ambassador. It was, indeed, through Fowler that Walsingham was able to keep in close touch with all Mauvissière's dealings with Scotland and with the Queen of Scots; but although he acquired a considerable mass of miscellaneous information by tapping both Mauvissière's correspondence and the letters of de Mainville, the official French envoy in Scotland, Walsingham seemed to be getting no nearer to solving the riddle of the 'great and hidden treason'.

The first real break came at the end of April 1583. By this time the English intelligence service had another spy operating inside the French embassy. This was a Frenchman, Henry Fagot (which may or may not have been his true name), who succeeded in suborning one of the ambassador's secretaries to betray his master, and from then on Walsingham received copies of practically every letter which passed between Mauvissière and Mary Queen of Scots. More importantly, it was information received from Henry Fagot which finally put the Secretary of State on the right track by drawing his attention to the suspicious behaviour of Francis Throckmorton, one of the Queen of Scots' chief agents, who haunted the French ambassador's house but seemed curiously shy of being seen in daylight.

Francis Throckmorton had been one of those eager young Catholic gentlemen recruited by Father Parsons to act as assistants to his missionary priests, and when Henry Fagot reported on 29 April that Mr Throckmorton had arranged to send the Queen of Scots the sum of 1,500 crowns, for which the French ambassador was security, Walsingham had no hesitation in extending the scope of his operations to include a watch on Throckmorton's movements.

By early November enough evidence had been collected to justify an arrest, and Throckmorton was taken at his London house by Paul's Wharf, where a number of incriminating papers were also seized. These included a list of prominent Catholic noblemen and gentlemen; plans of certain havens suitable 'for landing foreign forces'; a dozen copies of *The Descent of the Crown of England*, printed and published by the Bishop of Ross, in the defence of the pretended title of the Scottish Queen his mistress; plus 'certain infamous libels against her Majesty, printed and published beyond the seas'.

At his preliminary examination before the Council, Throckmorton tried to brazen things out, 'impudently' affirming that the maps of the harbours had been planted among his papers at the time of his arrest. Being 'more earnestly pressed to confess the truth', he said they had been left in his chamber, 'he knew not how', by a man of his called Nutby who had now fled the country. According to the official account, Throckmorton's interrogators, 'some of the principal personages of her Majesty's most honourable privy council', urged him 'in very mild and charitable manner' to confess the truth, but no persuasion prevailing,

> her Majesty thought it agreeable with good policy . . . to commit him over to the hands of some of her learned counsel, and others her faithful servants and ministers, with commission to them, to assay by torture to draw from him the truth of the matters appearing so weighty as to concern the invading of the realm.

Francis Throckmorton endured his first 'assay' with commendable resolution, continuing in 'his former obstinacy and denial of the truth', but when, three days later, he was put to the rack for a second time, 'before he was strained up to any purpose, he yielded to confess any thing he knew.' He told the commissioners appointed to examine him that the Duke of Guise was to be the principal commander and leader of the projected invasion; that its ostensible objective 'which should be publicly notified', was to release the Queen of Scots and to procure from the Queen's Majesty, if necessary by force, a measure of religious toleration for the English Catholics, but that the invaders were actually resolved, 'upon the Queen's Majesty's resistance, to remove her Majesty from her crown and state.' The Spanish ambassador had promised that the King his master would not only make some notable attempt against England, 'but also would bear half the charge of the enterprise.' The foreign forces were in readiness, and Francis Throckmorton, together with his brother Thomas, had undertaken to mobilize 'a convenient party' from among the English confederates to receive and join with them. This task was to be tackled with the help of the Spanish ambassador, for Throckmorton himself 'would not be seen to be a sounder of men' in case he aroused suspicion and so endangered the enterprise. But the ambassador, being a public figure, might, it was felt, 'safely deal therein'. The Duke of Guise, after rejecting several suggested landing places, had finally settled on the Sussex coast, 'about Arundel in Sussex', and had sent Charles Paget over 'to view the havens and country . . . and specially to sound and confer with certain principal persons for assistance.'

Full though it was, Throckmorton's confession was by no means complete. He had not been in on the conspiracy from the beginning and, in any case, had never played more than a subordinate part. But it was enough to give Walsingham the clue to the mystery of the 'great treason' which had defeated him for so long, and enabled him to start rounding up further suspects. In fact, the haul proved disappointingly meagre, since most of those named in Throckmorton's statement were already overseas or had been able to flee the realm in time – only the Earl of Northumberland, Lord Henry Howard, and Mr William Shelley of Michelgrove, a well-known recusant, were arrested, and only Francis Throckmorton later suffered the death penalty for high treason.

Another casualty of the affair was the Spanish ambassador, caught in the act of abusing his diplomatic privileges. Early in the new year Bernardino de Mendoza was summoned before the Council and brusquely informed that he was no longer *persona grata* with the Queen. His departure at the end of January in a flurry of mutual umbrage did not have much effect on the course of Anglo-Spanish relations – certainly his presence in England had done little or nothing to improve them. What did bring the inevitable confrontation perceptibly closer was the assassination on 1 July 1584 of William of Orange – shot three times at close range as he was going up the stairs of his house in Delft by a Burgundian, Balthazar Gérard, widely believed to have been an agent of the Spanish government.

The untimely death of the Prince of Orange meant that Dutch resistance to the Spanish army of occupation, now commanded by the able and energetic Duke of Parma, would almost certainly collapse – unless, of course, help came from outside – and Queen Elizabeth was brought face to face with an issue she had been successfully avoiding for nearly twenty years. Should she continue to stand aside, and see the remainder of Flanders, Holland and Zealand swallowed up and the whole of the North Sea coastline, with its vital embarkation ports, fall into Spanish hands; or should she embroil herself in a Continental war which would not only cost a great deal of money she could ill afford, but provide the King of Spain with an unassailable *casus belli* any time he cared to use it?

While the Queen and Council considered the international implications of William's death, other people were looking at it from a rather more personal angle. Two of the great European Protestant leaders – Admiral Coligny and the Prince of Orange – had now been murdered by Catholic fanatics. Now only Elizabeth was left. But for how long? The previous October a young Catholic gentleman named Somerville, or Somerfield, had set out for London from Warwickshire with the declared intention of shooting the Queen and seeing her head set on a pole, 'for she was a serpent and a viper.' There seems no reason to believe that Somerville was part of any larger scheme, and no doubt he was more than a little mad, but that did not necessarily make him any the less dangerous, as the twentieth century has good reason to know. It only needed one madman, one fanatic armed with knife or pistol, to get within range for a few vital seconds and the whole elaborate structure of Elizabethan government would have been destroyed literally at a stroke. There would be no Parliament – it was automatically dissolved on the death of the sovereign – no Privy Council, no lords lieutenant, no judges, no magistrates, no royal officials of any kind – their commissions all expired with the sovereign. There would, in fact, have been no authority anywhere until the heir-at-law took possession of the kingdom – and that heir was still the Queen of Scotland.

The danger was real enough. There was little doubt in London that the Pope would cheerfully have granted absolution to anyone who succeeded in sending 'that guilty woman of England' out of the world. In 1581 a renegade priest named Tyrrel had confessed to having heard the Holy Father say that such a deed would be 'a good work', and the matter had certainly been actively discussed by a variety of would-be assassins and the papal Secretary of State during the early 1580s. Elizabeth was not assassinated, but she easily might have been – there were plenty of shady characters flitting to and fro between England and the Continent throughout the reign with nothing to lose and everything, including a martyr's crown, to gain by a single climactic 'deed of violence'. The fact that she survived was surely due in part to the singular ineptitude of her ill-wishers and in part to the unsleeping vigilance of Francis Walsingham.

The Council, who knew more than most about the inside story, took the threat very seriously indeed, and when Parliament met at the end of November 1584 the members of the House of Commons found some difficulty in containing their loyalty, their patriotism and their fury against any person or persons 'by whom or for whom any such detestable act shall be attempted or committed'. Walter Mildmay, speaking in the debate on a bill intended to provide for the Queen's safety, scarcely needed to remind his hearers of the blessings of peace – 'now full twenty-six years, the like whereof, so long together, hath not been seen in any age' – which they had enjoyed by the ministry of their gracious Queen. Nor did he need further to chill their blood by spelling out the inevitable consequences of a successful 'sacred enterprise' – fuller details of which had just come to light from documents in the possession of Father Creighton, captured at sea by the Dutch acting on a tip-off from Walsingham. Quite as clearly as Sir Walter, the House of Commons could visualize the 'devastation of whole counties, sacking, spoiling and burning of cities and towns and villages, murdering of all kind of people without respect of person, age or sex, and so the ruin, subversion and conquest of this noble realm.'

Into this highly charged atmosphere the shocking revelations of the Parry Plot burst with predictably incendiary effect. Early in February 1585 Edmund Neville, himself a character of questionable loyalty, denounced William Parry, Doctor at Law, who he said had recently approached him with a scheme for killing the Queen so as to deliver the country from her 'bad and tyrannous government'.

According to Neville's statement, Parry had told him it would be a simple matter to come upon Elizabeth while she was walking, as was her custom, very privately in the palace gardens, shoot or stab her and then escape by a waiting barge downriver under cover of the general confusion.

William Parry had at one point in his colourful career been employed by Lord Burghley on secret-service work, and had gone abroad to try and penetrate 'the dangerous practices devised and attempted against her Majesty by her disloyal subjects and other malicious persons in foreign parts.' In the course of his duties, which had taken him to various centres in France from where he reported back on the movements of the English Catholic exiles, he had encountered Mary Stewart's agent Thomas Morgan, who suggested that he should undertake to murder Elizabeth. Parry replied that this 'might easily be done, if it might appear to be lawful', and had written off to Rome requesting papal approval for his 'Design'. He had returned to England at the beginning of 1584 and at once made a full report to the Queen, who heard him 'without being daunted' and subsequently granted him several marks of favour. Certain of his past misdeeds (including attempted murder and a conviction for burglary) were forgiven and he was actually sitting in the Parliament of 1584 as member for Queenborough. In December, however, he had shocked the House by making a speech in defence of the Jesuits, for which strange lapse of taste he had been committed to the serjeant's ward by his outraged colleagues and only released after his own abject apologies and the Queen's personal intervention.

When Parry was arrested he began by denying 'with great and vehement protestations' that he had been planning the Queen's destruction, but after a night's reflection – a night spent at Walsingham's house – and a confrontation with Edmund Neville, he changed his mind and eventually made a full confession without the added incentive of torture. But while admitting the truth of Neville's statement, he swore that he had never meant any harm to the Queen – on the contrary, he had been trying to uncover further plots against her life.

Dr Parry may have been an honest witness, in which case his only crime was over enthusiasm. But he was now no longer in government service and in the climate of the 1580s it would have been inviting disaster for a private individual even to mention a murder plot to anybody without authority from above. Also, if Parry had been acting the part of *agent provocateur* on his own initiative, it seems strange that he did not unburden himself to Francis Walsingham, as he had every opportunity to do at his first interrogation by Walsingham alone. Perhaps, as *Holinshed's Chronicle* grimly suggests, he had been practising 'at sundry times to have executed his most devilish purpose and determination; yet covering the same so much as in him lay with a veil and pretence of great loyalty unto her Majesty.'

William Parry remains something of an enigma. 'A man of very mean and base parentage but of a most proud and insolent spirit, bearing himself always far above the measure of his fortune after he had long led a wasteful and dissolute life', he was a typical product of that underworld of spies, adventurers and soldiers of fortune living by their wits, ready to sell their services and their souls to the highest bidder, resorting to straightforward crime when times were bad, hobnobbing with the great when their luck was in. Parry may have been a victim – he swore on the scaffold that he died a true servant of Queen Elizabeth. He may have been a double agent. He may have been engaging in a spot of private enterprise in the hope of collecting a reward – he was, like most of his kind, chronically short of cash and may simply have been seeking a way out his most pressing financial difficulties.

To the general public, by far the most startling disclosure of the affair (apart from the fact that so desperate a character was apparently able to have a private audience with the Queen just for the asking) was the letter addressed to Parry by the Cardinal of Como which was produced in evidence at his trial. In this remarkable document the papal secretary offered Pope Gregory's blessing, plenary indulgence and comprehensive good wishes for the success of Dr Parry's 'most holy and honourable purposes'. The Vatican thus provided the English government with a valuable propaganda weapon which it naturally exploited to the full, hurrying into print with a pamphlet on the subject and issuing special prayers of thanksgiving for the Queen's miraculous escape, while in the House of Commons, where the members were busy trying to safeguard the Queen by making it clear in the strongest possible terms that the Catholic heiress would not survive to enjoy an inheritance seized for her by violent means, a motion was made 'with a general applause of the whole House' to revive the attempt to start judicial proceedings against the Queen of Scots first propounded at the time of the Ridolfi plot thirteen years earlier.

No one was suggesting that Mary had had any prior knowledge of William Parry's dubious purposes, but equally no one doubted that she had known about and approved all the details of the so-called Throckmorton plot. Certainly Francis Walsingham never doubted it, and he was in the best position to know. In 1572 Walsingham had written to the Earl of Leicester that 'so long as that devilish woman lives, neither her Majesty must make account to continue in quiet possession of her crown, nor her faithful servants assure themselves of safety of their lives.' Everything which had happened since had served only to confirm that opinion, and her Majesty's faithful Secretary of State now began to bend all his considerable energies to the task of finding a final solution to the problem of the Queen of Scotland. Mary had already been removed from the Earl of Shrewsbury's charge – to Francis Walsingham one of the more disturbing revelations of the Throckmorton affair had been the ease with which Mary was apparently able to send and receive uncensored letters in the large, laxly supervised Shrewsbury establishments, and he had for some time been urging the need for a general tightening of security. It was certainly time for a change. The Earl himself was begging to be relieved of an increasingly 'cumbersome' and thankless burden, and in the summer of 1584 the Queen of Scots' involvement in a rancorous Shrewsbury family quarrel which threatened to become a public scandal had given the authorities an unexceptionable excuse for transferring her to the custody of a new 'keeper'.

This was Sir Amyas Paulet, a close and trusted friend of Francis Walsingham and well known to share his strict Puritanical principles. He treated Mary with scrupulous respect but was immune to her famous charm, and under his stern regime the last shreds of face-saving pretence that she was anything other than a political prisoner rapidly disappeared.

Paulet took over in April 1585 and began as he meant to go on, telling Mary that he would not be diverted from his duty 'by hope of gain, fear of loss, or for any other respect whatsoever'. He told Walsingham that he would never ask pardon if she escaped

by any treacherous slight or cunning device . . . My conscience beareth me witness and my doing I hope shall testify for me, that

91

as I have been very careful and curious to perform every syllable contained in my instructions . . . so I have done all my endeavour to make these people and their friends to know that if it were possible I would not be deceived by them.

Paulet's instructions had been drafted by Walsingham personally and were extremely detailed. There was to be no communication between Mary's retinue (which still numbered more than forty persons) and Paulet's own servants, except in his presence; none of Mary's servants were to leave the house without an escort; no strangers were to be admitted on any pretext whatever and special attention was to be paid to the comings and goings of 'laundresses, coachmen and the like', who, it was believed, had previously acted as unofficial postmen.

It was an essential part of Walsingham's strategy that Mary should henceforward be effectively isolated from the outside world and all through the spring and summer of 1585 Paulet was engaged in methodically stopping the earths. 'I have (I thank God) reformed no small number of abuses of dangerous consequence', he wrote, 'and experience doth inform me daily of other such new faults as might carry great peril, which I omit not to redress by little and little as I may.' Mary's official correspondence with the French ambassador was now being quite openly read by Paulet before it was delivered, and in September she was told that in future any packets she wished to send to her correspondents in France must be handed to her gaolers instead of being forwarded direct to the embassy in London. Just before Christmas the Queen of Scots was moved to Chartley in Staffordshire – a large, moated manor house belonging to the young Earl of Essex – and early in the New Year Paulet was able to report that he now believed it was impossible for a piece of paper as big as his finger to be conveyed without his knowledge. Stage one of the plan had been successfully completed and it was time to put stage two into operation.

In December 1585 a Catholic exile named Gilbert Gifford had come over from France, entrusted by Thomas Morgan with the task of trying to find a way of evading Paulet's vigilance and re-opening a channel of communication with Mary. Gifford had first gone abroad in or about 1577 and two years later, at the age of nineteen, had entered the English College at Rome as a candidate for the priesthood. He did not last the course, and spent most of the early 1580s leading a gipsy-like existence wandering round Europe and visiting England on at least one occasion. In the autumn of 1583 he surfaced again, penniless and apparently penitent, at the doors of William Allen's English College, now established at Rheims in northern France. After some hesitation, Dr Allen admitted him to the seminary, where he stayed for the next two years, a seemingly reformed character. But in October 1585 he left for Paris, where he made contact with Thomas Morgan and Charles Paget and was soon deeply involved in the faction fighting which divided the exile community. Gifford, like Morgan and Paget, aligned himself with the 'seculars', that is supporters of the secular, seminary-trained priests, against the religious orders, specifically the Jesuits, who looked like threatening to take over total command of the English mission field.

There is, not surprisingly, no proof that Gilbert Gifford was Walsingham's mole during his sojourn at Rheims, but the presumption must be pretty strong. Certainly, his return to England looks, in the circumstances, a little too convenient to have been entirely coincidental. At any rate, he was arrested immediately on his arrival at the port of Rye and sent straight to London where he spent some time in secret conference with the Secretary, who put certain propositions to him.

Francis Walsingham, it appeared, was as anxious as Thomas Morgan to re-establish the Queen of Scots' private post office. This time, though, it would be a supervised private post office. The arrangements discussed between Gifford, Walsingham and Walsingham's confidential assistant Thomas Phelippes, were ingenious but essentially simple. Beer for the household at Chartley was delivered once a week from the nearby town of Burton. With the connivance of the brewer, letters could be carried in and out in a watertight container, a leather bag or box small enough to be inserted into the bung-hole of a beer barrel. Gifford's role would be to collect Mary's personal mail from the French embassy, where it arrived by diplomatic bag. He would then pass it to Thomas Phelippes, an expert linguist and genius with codes. While Phelippes deciphered and translated the letters, Gifford would make his way to Chartley and wait until the originals were returned to him by Paulet. He would then hand them to the brewer and the brewer, unknown to Gifford, would take them back to Paulet, who could thus check that nothing had been added to the package, which was then sent in by beer barrel as arranged. The outgoing post would work in reverse order – Gifford would get it from the brewer and hand it to Paulet, who in turn would send it on to Walsingham. Gifford, meanwhile, returned to London and would, in due course, deliver Mary's letters to the French ambassador. The trap looked foolproof and Walsingham undoubtedly hoped that it would prove to be a death trap.

Thomas Phelippes travelled up to Chartley at the end of December to confer with Amyas Paulet and also to arrange matters with the brewer, while Gilbert Gifford in London had to make himself known to the French ambassador and gain his confidence. Gifford had come provided with letters of recommendation from Thomas Morgan and the ambassador, Chateauneuf, who had succeeded Mauvissière the previous September, apparently saw no reason to doubt him when he explained 'his' plan for communicating with the Queen of Scotland.

The first trial delivery was made on 16 January 1586 and went without a hitch. It is not clear who, or by what means, Mary herself was informed of the re-opening of communications but she was naturally delighted to have made contact once again with the world of intrigue which was her lifeline, and gave orders that the backlog of clandestine correspondence which had been piling up at the French embassy should be sent on to her forthwith. Eighteen years earlier Francis Knollys had written of the Queen of Scots, 'she hath courage enough to hold out as long as any foot of hope may be left unto her', and she had not changed.

To start with, the person who derived most benefit from this unusual postal service was the brewer from Burton, code-named 'the honest man'. He was, of course, being handsomely paid for his trouble by both parties to the transaction but, as a man of sound business instincts, it soon occurred to him to raise the price of his invaluable beer. Paulet considered his demands both peremptory and unreasonable, but was obliged to give in to them 'or lose his service.'

Meanwhile, an exceptional amount of overtime was being worked in Walsingham's office as letters, twenty-one packets of them 'great and small', some of which had been awaiting delivery for nearly two years, started to emerge from the French ambassador's private coffers. These packets could not, of course, be inserted in the bung hole post-box as they were and had to be divided up into more manageable lots for delivery. This provided a plausible excuse for breaking the seals. Walsingham, or one of his underlings, had long since perfected a method of opening a letter without appearing to disturb its seal, but it was obviously helpful not to have to go to so much trouble when dealing with correspondence on such a large scale.

By the end of February 1586 Francis Walsingham was in a position to read practically every letter written to Mary by her friends since the breaking of the Throckmorton plot. There were letters from her agents in the Low Countries, from Thomas Morgan and the Archbishop of Glasgow in Paris, from Charles Paget and Sir Francis Englefield, from Robert Parsons, from the Duke of Guise and the Duke of Parma. Together they provided a complete picture of all that Mary's partisans in Europe had been doing and saying on her behalf during the past two years. It was the sort of windfall which every secret-service chief dreams of; but although it filled many gaps in his knowledge and gave him much interesting information to be filed for future reference, it did not in general terms tell Walsingham much that he had not already known from other sources or been able to guess at.

By the middle of May, Mary's replies were beginning to come back. In them she made it perfectly clear that she sympathized fully with the Queen's enemies, that she would welcome an invasion of England, whether Guisard, Spanish or both, and was willing and eager to snatch her cousin's throne. All this was useful corroborative evidence regarding Mary's general attitude, but again told Walsingham little that he did not already know. From past experience the Secretary also knew that the only hope of persuading Elizabeth to proceed 'to extremity' against the Queen of Scots would be by presenting her with detailed, incontrovertible proof that her heir was actively plotting against her life. He was by no means unhopeful that such proof would presently be forthcoming and in the meantime the beer barrels were providing him with a first-rate listening post.

The genesis of the Babington plot, like that of its numerous predecessors, is complicated and more than somewhat obscure. In a labyrinth of spy and counter-spy, double agent and agent provocateur, it is far from clear who was double-crossing who. It is also evident that it was often far from clear at the time. In outline, though, the plot was the mixture as before – a rising of the English Catholics, aided by an invading army financed jointly by Spain and the Pope, the release of the Queen of Scots, the removal of Elizabeth and the 'restoration of religion'.

Two things, however, gave this particular affair its distinctive character. One was the fact that the assassination of Elizabeth – 'the despatch of the usurping competitor' – formed an integral part of the plan from the beginning. (Some conspirators had been less explicit on this point, but of course the death of Elizabeth had always been an essential precondition for the success of any plot to raise Mary to her throne.) The other fact was that on this occasion, thanks to the beer-barrel post, the English government was able to follow developments from a very early stage.

Bernardino de Mendoza, now *en poste* at the Spanish embassy in Paris, Thomas Morgan and Charles Paget were all more or less involved. On 11 May Mendoza reported to Philip that he had received a visit from a priest (his name was John Ballard), who came on behalf of the principal English Catholics

'to say that God has infused more courage then ever into them, and has opened their eyes to the fact that no time is so opportune as the present to shake off the oppression of the Queen and the yoke of heresy that weighs upon them . . . . They say that, as I have never yet deceived them, they beg me to tell them whether your Majesty had determined to help them to take up arms when they decided to do so.

At about the same time Mendoza dispatched a highly confidential message, written and ciphered by him personally, which was to be put into the King's own hand:

I am advised from England by four men of position who have the run of the Queen's house, that they have discussed for the last three months the intention of killing her . . . . they will on the first opportunity advise me when it is to be done, and whether by poison or steel, in order that I may send the intelligence to your Majesty, supplicating you to be pleased to help them after the business is effected.

The priest John Ballard was already known to Walsingham. Originally a Cambridge man, he had come to England from Rheims in the early summer of 1581 and for the next few years had followed the perilous calling of a missionary priest, wandering from place to place under a variety of aliases. In May 1585 he was reported to be in London, lodging at one of 'the common inns', and in August of that year the agent Nicholas Berden, otherwise Thomas Rogers, wrote to Walsingham from France warning that Ballard was one of the chief trouble-makers among the disaffected Catholic nobility. Thus alerted, Walsingham began to take a close interest in John Ballard, or Captain Fortesque as he was most often known. According to William Camden, when Ballard went over to see Mendoza he was accompanied by one of Walsingham's spies, Barnard or Bernard Maude, 'a notable crafty Dissembler, who had egregiously deceived the unwary Priest' and who, again according to Camden, wrung from him all his secrets. Maude, and another of Walsingham's agents, Captain Jakhous or Jacques, were later accused by Edward Windsor, one of the young men more or less implicated in Babington's treason, of having played the part of *agents provocateurs*, and it seems at least highly likely that Walsingham knew a good deal about Ballard's plans by the time he returned from France in the spring of 1586.

Ballard went at once to London, where he made contact with a group of ardent young Catholic gentlemen who hung about the fringes of the Court and in particular with one of their leaders, Anthony Babington, scion of a wealthy Derbyshire family, good-looking, charming, vain and fatally lacking in the qualities which make a successful conspirator. Babington had first made the acquaintance of the Queen of Scots in the days when he had been a page in the Earl of Shrewsbury's household, where he had on several occasions acted as one of her unofficial postmen. A zealous Catholic with his head stuffed with romantic notions, he had gained the reputation among Mary's friends abroad for being one of her staunchest supporters, and seemed the obvious person to be entrusted with organizing her actual rescue.

According to Babington's own story, Ballard came to him in his lodgings in Holborn towards the end of May and proceeded to outline a grandiose scheme, which he said was in active preparation, for an invasion by a Catholic army 60,000 strong. Babington was sceptical; he could not imagine how the Catholic powers would raise so many men in so short a time – before the end of the summer, according to Ballard – or have the means to transport them. Besides this, he thought 'their assistance on this side small . . . so long as her Majesty doth live, the State being so well settled.' Ballard's reply came pat. 'He answered that difficulty would be taken away by means already laid, and that her life could be no

97

hindrance therein.' The 'means already laid', it appeared, was an oath sworn by John Savage to undertake the murder of Queen Elizabeth. Savage, another Catholic exile, had been at Rheims the previous summer, when a plot to assassinate Elizabeth had been discussed with Gilbert Gifford, his cousin Dr William Gifford and a priest Christopher Hodgson. Savage, who had had a brief career as a mercenary in the Duke of Parma's army, was cast in the role of first murderer and had come over to England in August 1585 for that very purpose, but his courage failed him and now the poison chalice was being passed to Anthony Babington.

Over the next few weeks Babington embarked on a series of intellectually stimulating but not especially productive discussions with his friends concerning the 'lawfulness' or otherwise of assassinating the Queen and its likely effect on the fortunes of the English Catholics. John Ballard had gone north to take further soundings among the Catholic gentry, still accompanied by Bernard Maude, and while he was away Babington acquired his own shadow in the person of Robert Poley or Pooley, who held a minor office at Court, but whose more important occupation was that of secret agent. Poley made a speciality of insinuating himself into the intimate acquaintance of the London Catholic community and had gained the reputation of being 'a worthy man, both honourable and devout'. Thomas Morgan trusted him and so, fatally, did Anthony Babington, who was soon confiding freely in his new friend.

Significantly, this appears to have been the moment chosen by Walsingham to send in through the beer barrel post a letter from Thomas Morgan dated 29 April, telling Mary that he had been dealing with Babington on her behalf, that Babington was 'somewhat jealous' – that is, disappointed – at not having heard from her for such a long time, and advising her to write him a friendly letter. This she did on 25 June. On 7 July no less a person than Thomas Phelippes left London for Chartley carrying Babington's reply, which was addressed to his 'most dread Sovereign Lady and Queen' and contained a detailed exposition of the plans currently afoot for her release and rehabilitation. From Francis Walsingham's point of view the most interesting paragraph came towards the end. Babington had written:

For the despatch of the usurper, from the obedience of whom we are by the excommunication of her made free, there be six noble gentlemen all my private friends, who for the zeal they bear unto the Catholic cause and your majesty's service will undertake that tragical execution. It resteth that according to their good deserts and your majesty's bounty their heroical attempt may be honourably rewarded in them if they escape with life, or in their posterity and that so much I may be able by your majesty's authority to assure them.

This, of course, is what Walsingham had been waiting and hoping for. Everything now depended on Mary's reply, and Thomas Phelippes waited at Chartley to be ready at hand to decipher it the moment it emerged from the beer barrels. First, on 13 July, there was a brief acknowledgement from the Queen of Scots' French secretary, Claude Nau. 'We attend her very heart at the next' wrote Phelippes to Walsingham on 14 July. Three days later, on 17 July, it came.

It was a very long letter. After warmly commending Babington and his plans in general terms, Mary went on to offer the conspirators much sound practical advice on how 'to ground substantially this enterprise and to bring it to good success.' For example, they must consider carefully

what forces as well on foot as on horse you may raise amongst you all and what captains you shall appoint for them in every shire . . . what place you esteem fittest to assemble the principal company of your forces . . . what foreign forces, as well on horse as foot you require, for how long paid and munitioned and what ports are fittest for their landing in this realm . . . by what means do the six gentlemen deliberate to proceed . . . also the manner of my getting forth of this hold.

Mary was especially anxious that there should be 'no stirring on this side' until the provision of foreign aid was assured and, above all, that the strictest security should be observed: 'Take heed of spies and false brethren that are amongst you, and in any wise keep never any paper about you that in any sort may do harm.' Failure to take such elementary precautions had been the downfall of so many who had 'heretofore travailed in like occasions', and the Queen of Scots, knowing that if anything went wrong this time the consequences were liable to be disastrous, not only for Babington and his friends but for herself, 'it were sufficient cause given to that Queen [Elizabeth] in catching me again, to enclose me forever in some

99

hole, forth of the which I should never escape, if she did use me no worse', was understandably emphatic that there should be no leaks, that no detail of the preliminary staffwork should be neglected. She wrote:

> Affairs being thus prepared, and forces in readiness both without and within the realm, then shall it be time to set the six gentlemen to work, taking order, upon the accomplishing of their design, I may be suddenly transported out of this place, and that all your forces in the same time be on the field to meet me in tarrying for the arrival of the foreign aid, which then must be hastened with all diligence.

If this did not sign Mary's death warrant then nothing would; but Walsingham, in his natural anxiety to make a clean sweep of the conspirators, either instructed or allowed Thomas Phelippes – who included the art of forgery among his other talents – to add a postscript asking for 'the names and qualities of the six gentlemen that are to accomplish the designment' before the letter, sometimes known as 'the bloody letter', was forwarded to its destination. He thus provided useful ammunition for all those partisans of Mary who were later to insist that she had been framed.

As it turned out, it was a waste of effort and Walsingham came perilously close to ruining everything by waiting for a reply which never came. He wrote to Phelippes on 3 August,

> I think if the messenger receive not answer this day at Babington's hands, then were it not good to defer the apprehension of him, lest he should escape. If you hope, by giving of time, that an answer will be drawn from him, then wish I the stay. It may be that the deferring of the answer proceedeth upon conference [among the conspirators] which, if it be so, then were it a great hindrance of the service to proceed over hastily to the arrest. These causes are subject to so many difficulties as it is a hard matter to resolve. Only this I conclude, it were better to lack the answer than to lack the man.

Walsingham was keeping in contact with Babington through Robert Pooley and had actually had some meetings with him earlier in July, when Babington had spoken of his desire to travel abroad and offered his services as a spy! Finally, on 4 August orders were given for the arrests to begin. John Ballard was the first to be taken, news of which seems at last to have roused Babington to a sense of his own danger. Camden has a story that he invited Walsingham's servants to supper at an inn and escaped from them by pretending to go and pay the reckoning, leaving a valuable cloak and sword behind him. He fled to the then leafy glades of St John's Wood until driven by hunger to seek shelter at the house of a Catholic family named Bellamy living in the village of Harrow-on-the-Hill. Here Babington and two companions, Robert Barnwell and Henry Dunne, were cared for by the hospitable Bellamys. 'There were they hid in barns', says Camden, 'there were they fed and clothed in rude country habit. But the tenth day after they were discovered and brought up to London, the City testifying their public joy by ringing of bells, making of bonfires and singing of psalms.' The rest of the conspirators were picked up without much difficulty – John Savage, Chideock Tichborne, Charles Tilney, Thomas Salisbury, Edward Abington and John Charnock were all in custody by the middle of August.

Meanwhile, steps had been taken against the most important conspirator of them all. At the beginning of August William Waad, Clerk to the Privy Council, had travelled very secretly to Chartley to see Amyas Paulet, and the two men had talked out in the 'open fields' as a precaution against eavesdroppers. As a result of these discussions, a plan was agreed and on 11 August the Queen of Scots received an unexpected but welcome invitation to attend a stag hunt in Sir Walter Aston's park at neighbouring Tixall. She set out escorted by the omnipresent Amyas Paulet and a retinue which included her two secretaries, Claude Nau and Gilbert Curle, and nourishing who knows what hopes that this might be the prelude to her long-awaited rescue. On the road, the party was met by a troop of horsemen, but they were no rescuers. The two secretaries were arrested and Mary herself, protesting bitterly, was taken on to Tixall, where she was kept incommunicado while her rooms at Chartley were searched and her papers confiscated.

The breaking of the Babington plot may fairly be regarded as the culmination of Francis Walsingham's career as an intelligence chief, and there were (for that matter, there still are) those who maintained that the whole affair had been fabricated by him with the sole object of bringing about the undoing of the Queen of Scots. But while it is certainly true that Walsingham was dedicated to Mary's undoing, there is absolutely nothing to show that he was party to the discussions which had taken place at Rheims the previous summer between John Savage and the Giffords. It is, however, surely true that he knew of them once Gilbert Gifford had landed at Rye in December 1585. It is also true that Gifford continued to promote the plot and encourage the plotters with, it must be assumed, Walsingham's knowledge and consent. Gilbert Gifford, incidentally, was also playing a double, if not a triple game, betraying Walsingham's secrets back to Morgan and Paget in France under cover of reporting *their* secrets to London! According to some authorities, Morgan and Paget too were engaged in betraying the Queen of Scots, and there is good reason to believe that they were cheating her over the payment of her French dower income.

So, as far as it is possible to be certain of anything, it seems reasonable to surmise that a murder plot of sorts did exist, that Walsingham came to hear of it in its very early stages and allowed, more likely perhaps ensured, that it should develop to the point at which the Queen of Scots had implicated herself beyond the possibility of doubt. He was to receive some useful assistance from the conspirators themselves now in custody. According to William Camden, 'many days were spent in examining of them, who cut one another's throats by their confessions, and discovered the whole truth of the business.' Certainly, Babington seemed eager to make a clean breast of it, freely admitting everything to his interrogators, including the murder plot and his correspondence with Mary. The secretaries Nau and Curle also had no hesitation in selling their mistress down the river. Confronted with a copy of Mary's fatal last letter to Babington, they both agreed that it was substantially correct. Claude Nau deposed that he had made a fair copy in French from a draft or 'minute' drawn up by Mary herself. Walsingham had hoped and, much to his disappointment, failed to find this minute among the Queen of Scot's papers at Chartley. Gilbert Curle had made the English translation and put it into cipher. And not only the Babington letter. As he subsequently explained: 'They did show me her Majesty's letters to my lord Paget, Mr Charles Paget, Sir Francis Englefield and the Spanish ambassador, all penned in my own hand which I could not deny.'

At her trial Mary, understandably, attacked the authenticity of the Babington letter. When she heard it read before the panel of commissioners (which included Francis Walsingham) assembled in the great hall of Fotheringay Castle, she denounced it as a forgery. She went on to say that she feared this was Walsingham's work, who sought by this means to bring her to her death, and that she had heard of previous 'practices' of his against her life. This brought Walsingham to his feet. 'I call God to witness', he told the court, 'that as a private person I have done nothing unbeseeming an honest man, nor, as I bear the place of a public man, have I done anything unworthy of my place.' But, he confessed, that being very careful for the safety of the Queen and the realm, he had 'curiously searched out all the practices against the same.' As an intelligence chief, Walsingham may sometimes have bent the rules a little, but with an adversary of the calibre of the Queen of Scotland he surely had no need to fabricate plots.

CHAPTER FIVE

Sweet England's pride

———◆———

The breaking of the Babington plot had been a major coup for Queen Elizabeth's secret service, the subsequent trial and execution of that 'bosom serpent' the Queen of Scotland a personal triumph for spymaster Francis Walsingham, but the day-to-day work of the service continued, and continued to be much concerned with monitoring the activities of the Catholic underground at home and the Catholic exiles abroad.

The responsibility for discovering and apprehending the missionary priests and those who sheltered them was not Walsingham's alone, but was shared with the local authorities, civil and ecclesiastical. In fact, the routine business of dealing with the priests and religious dissidents was mostly left to the lords lieutenant of the counties, the magistrates and bishops, some of whom employed their own spies and searchers and all of whom relied heavily on the services of a countrywide network of free-lance informers who ranged from the semi-professional priest-catcher to zealous patriots seeing a 'pollyticke Jesuit' behind every bush, or just some disgruntled individual with a score to pay off.

Apart from the edicts and instructions periodically handed down by the Privy Council, the system operated with little or no central control, its success rate depending on the strength of local feeling, the sympathies of the local magnate, the energy of the local bishop. Overall, though, it was remarkably successful. In that small, close-knit society where everybody knew his neighbour's business, his politics and his religious leanings, and where no stranger could hope to pass unnoticed or unexplained, the great majority of the

104

missionaries were sooner or later picked up by the ordinary processes of law enforcement.

While Francis Walsingham naturally encouraged and approved of priest-catching at a local level, he was not directly connected with it, and used his own methods of gathering information about the organization of the missionaries and their movement from the foreign training colleges. Some of this information came from government sources in France, the Low Countries and Scotland, and some from the networks of semi-official, part-time agents scattered all over Europe; some came from regular diplomatic sources, in particular from the Paris embassy, and some again from enterprising individuals such as stationer's apprentice Anthony Munday, who had travelled to Rome itself and spent some time as a guest at the English College.

Walsingham was always interested in news or gossip, however trivial, about the doings of the expatriate Catholic community – who was consorting with whom, who had fallen out, who had gone on a journey, who seemed to have come into money or was planning to move house. His thirst for scraps of information of all kinds was well known on the international grapevine, as was his willingness to pay generous rates. He was particularly interested in news of the refugee colonies in Flanders and northern France, which often yielded valuable clues regarding the movement of priests already in England and the infiltration of new recruits, now being organized by Robert Parsons from his headquarters at Rouen.

There were, of course, government 'searchers' at all the main ports of entry in the south-east, but these officials were notoriously corrupt and, in any case, many of the missionaries were now being put across in small boats which could be beached on some lonely stretch of coast under cover of darkness. Walsingham is known to have employed a number of agents specifically to watch and track down priests working in England during the 1580s. The exact number is not known, but there are four men who can be definitely identified as being engaged exclusively in priest-hunting. They were Robert Barnard, who used the work name of P. H. and was operating in London and later in the north country between January and November 1582; Walter Williams, at one time a servant of one of the Catholic exiles in France; Maliverny Catlyn, a man of some education, who had been both a soldier and a scholar and seems to have belonged to a rather higher social class than the general run of

Walsingham's agents; and Thomas Rogers, more often known as Nicholas Berden. Berden was the most reliable and efficient of the English spies. He wrote to Thomas Phelippes in January 1584:

> I profess myself a spy, but am not one for gain but to serve my country. . . . Whensoever any occasion shall be offered wherein I may adventure some rare and desperate exploit such as may be for the honour of my country and my own credit, you shall always find me resolute and ready to perform the same.

Berden first appears in the record as being in the service of George Gilbert, a prominent and influential Catholic layman, and his principal usefulness to Walsingham lay in the wide range of his contacts among the Catholic community. Based in London in the spring of 1585, he was dining with 'Edmonds the Jesuit', otherwise Father William Weston, a leading member of the mission, who is credited with the conversion of Philip Howard, Earl of Arundel. Berden gave details of four or five houses in the capital which the Father was known to visit, and added the names of a number of other priests and Catholic gentlemen who were also said to resort to them. 'The Papists', he went on, 'do expect forty or fifty priests from Rome and Rheims to arrive here in England, which news Dr Allen's man did bring unto them, and with their coming I hope to be made acquainted.'

Berden wasted no time in furthering his acquaintance with Dr Allen's man, whose name was Richard. 'I demanded of the said Richard what means the priests had to come into England and who receives them at their first entry', he wrote on 13 April. 'He answered me that . . . the said priests most commonly do come over in French boats that come to Newcastle for coals.' It seemed that Robert Highcliffe, the Queen's officer at Newcastle, was 'a papist in heart', and he and his wife had organized a regular system for meeting the newcomers, sheltering them in the houses of sympathetic local gentry and providing them with transport for their journeys on to their various destinations. The unsuspecting Richard was also the source of valuable information regarding the current state of the illicit book trade – who was writing, who printing, importing and distributing works of Catholic propaganda. By posing as a customer, Berden was offered first choice of the latest titles, both by William Bray, named by Richard as one of the principal traffickers in banned books, and by Richard himself, who was hoping to bring a consignment over with him on his next visit to England.

In August 1585 Walsingham sent Berden over to Paris with instructions to widen his circle of friends among the exiles – especially those who had fled in the aftermath of the Throckmorton affair. Berden spent about eight months in France and was highly successful in gaining the confidence of the English Catholics there. When he returned, he was able to report that he had been

> thought meet to be employed by Charles Paget, Charles Arundel, Stephen Brinkley from Allen and Parsons, Godfrey Foljambe and Thomas Fitzherbert to be their correspondent here for the receiving and delivery of such letters as they shall send unto me, and to give them intelligence from England.

The Catholics appear to have had no doubt that Berden was one of them – indeed, his cover was so good that on his return from France he was obliged to ask for Walsingham's protection against Mr Justice Young, one of the most enthusiastic of the priest-catchers.

As a valued member of the service, his opinion was sometimes sought when the disposal of imprisoned priests was being considered. Those not destined for the gallows could be deported or sent to the concentration camp at Wisbech in Cambridgeshire, and it was part of Walsingham's brief to advise the Privy Council on any doubtful cases. Sometimes Berden would work to secure the release of a prisoner. He wrote to Thomas Phelippes in June 1586:

> if it please you to procure me the liberty of Ralph Bickley, seminary priest in the Gatehouse at his honour's hands it will be worth £20 to me; and the liberty also of Richard Sherwood alias Carlton, prisoner in the Counter in Wood Street, will be worth £30. . . . The money [he continued plaintively] will do me great pleasure, being now in extreme need thereof.

In November of the same year he was thanking Walsingham

> for that it pleased you to spare Christopher Dryland's life at the last sessions at my request. It has much increased my credit among the papists that by my endeavour his life was saved, for they suppose that some friend at my request moved your Honour therein.

Berden pursued his career as an undercover agent for about another year, when he retired to 'enter a more public course of life', applying for, and apparently receiving, a post in the palace catering department.

Berden had continued to correspond intermittently with the Paris exiles, and it was, in fact, belated doubts about his integrity raised in Paris in the spring of 1588 which finally caused Walsingham to dispense with the services of one of his most valuable agents. Paris, the centre of Guisard power and influence, where most of Mary Stewart's friends were to be found and where old purblind Mendoza at the Spanish embassy was still weaving his plots against the Protestant island, had always held a special interest for Francis Walsingham, and the embassy there represented a vital listening post. It was therefore unfortunate that grave suspicions should have existed regarding the loyalty of Queen Elizabeth's ambassador, Sir Edward Stafford, who held the post from 1583 to 1587.

Edward Stafford was very highly connected. Descended from both the Stafford Dukes of Buckingham and the aristocratic Pole family, he had inherited a double ration of royal Plantagenet genes; his mother, Dorothy, was a personal friend of the Queen and his wife, Douglas Sheffield, had been born a Howard. But Stafford was chronically hard up – he seems to have been in debt all his life – and his family background naturally inclined him towards a conservative view of religion and politics. He was certainly out of sympathy with the aggressive Protestant fundamentalism of Leicester and Walsingham and never troubled to conceal his distaste for the radical element on the Privy Council.

Walsingham, for his part, neither liked nor trusted the blue-blooded diplomat. He strongly suspected Stafford's secretary of supplying classified information to Thomas Morgan, and Michael Moody, another of the embassy servants, of smuggling letters from the Catholic exiles in France to their friends at home. By the spring of 1585 he had begun to suspect Stafford himself of being on dangerously confidential terms with men like the Paget brothers and Charles Arundel, so that when Nicholas Berden crossed the Channel that summer his instructions included a commission to keep a discreet eye on the ambassador's activities.

Berden's reports appeared to confirm Walsingham's suspicions that the embassy was being used as a post office by the Catholic expatriates, adding that Charles Arundel was able to send any man into England 'by the ambassador's means'. More seriously, it seemed that 'the Lord Ambassador, in consideration of 6,000 crowns . . . did show to the Duke of Guise his letters of intelligence out of England.' And not only the Duke of Guise. In January 1587 Mendoza told King Philip that Stafford had sent Charles Arundel to see him 'to ascertain from your Majesty in what way he might serve you.' The ambassador, Mendoza went on, was known to be much pressed for money, 'and even if he had not made such an offer as this, his poverty is reason enough to expect from him any service, if he saw it was to be remunerated.' Before Mendoza had time to sign this dispatch, Arundel was once again on the doorstep with news from Edward Stafford that an English fleet was about to sail against Portugal.

> The ambassador told Arundel to advise your Majesty of this instantly, which, he said, would serve as a sample and handsel of his goodwill; and within a fortnight or three weeks he would report whether the despatch of the fleet was being persisted in, together with the exact number of ships, men, stores and all other details of the project.

Mendoza thought that, although the ambassador seemed only too willing to part with information, it would nevertheless be advisable to offer him some tangible token of Spanish regard, and in a letter dated 27 February Philip authorized the payment of 2,000 crowns to this valuable 'new correspondent'.

The evidence against Stafford looks conclusive at first glance, but in the looking glass world of spy and countery-spy things are seldom what they appear at first glance, and the case against the ambassador has never been proved conclusively. He may indeed have been betraying his trust and high position and selling his country's secrets to the enemy for money at a time of great national danger. On the other hand, he may, as he himself always maintained, have simply been feeding the enemy false information and deliberately posing as a traitor to men like Arundel, Guise and even Bernardino de Mendoza in order to discover their secrets: 'I mean to use them all well', he had told Walsingham at the beginning of his embassy; 'For my part I am minded to use the Devil himself well if he could come to me in the likeness of a man, to serve the Queen withal.' Walsingham was never sufficiently sure of his ground to risk accusing Stafford openly, knowing that the evidence of spies such as Nicholas Berden and Gilbert Gifford would have carried little weight against a man of Stafford's standing in society. Instead he made discreet use of the ambassador as a channel of misinformation to the enemy.

As the decade progressed, so the threat from Spain grew more obvious and the energies of Walsingham's secret service were accordingly being concentrated on intelligence gathering in that quarter. Philip's naval preparations were, of course, there for all to see who had business in the Spanish ports. Every sea captain and merchant trader had his tale to tell, and it was common knowledge in every dockside tavern that the King of Spain was assembling a great invasion fleet against the heretic Queen of England.

But Francis Walsingham wanted more than sailors' gossip. He wanted details of tonnage, of ordnance, powder and ball, numbers of soldiers, sailors and galley slaves, of the quantities of provisions, biscuit, salt fish, oil and wine being collected for the fleet. At about the time Francis Drake was setting off on his beard-singeing expedition to Cadiz, Walsingham was drawing up an *aide mémoire* headed 'A Plot for Intelligence out of Spain'. Edward Stafford in Paris was to find out as much as he could from his Venetian counterpart (the Venetians had a name for being exceptionally well informed), and contact was to be established with the French ambassador in Madrid. A reliable correspondent in Rouen was to be instructed to collect regular news reports from travellers reaching Nantes, Le Havre and Dieppe from Spain, while two 'special persons' – French, Flemings or Italians – were to be selected to go down the Spanish coast 'to see what preparations are a-making there.' Also – and vitally important – up-to-date and reliable intelligence must be obtained both from the Spanish court and the Duke of Parma's headquarters at Brussels.

Walsingham had at least one experienced agent in Parma's camp – Edward Burnham had already had a long and adventurous career in the service, including three months in Portugal exposed to daily risk of arrest – and, despite all the dangers and difficulties involved, there were English spies in Spain itself. One of these, Nicholas Ousley, was living in Malaga. Bernardino de Mendoza knew of his presence there in July 1587, when he told King Philip that Walsingham had described Ousley as 'one of the cleverest men he knew', adding that the Queen was very much indebted to him for his regular, trustworthy information. Ousley evaded the Spanish authorities and was still sending his trustworthy reports to London as late as April 1588. He served in the English fleet as a volunteer on the *Revenge* in the Armada campaign and was eventually rewarded for having adventured his life in so many ways in the Queen's service with a grant of the lease of the parsonage of St Helen's Bishopsgate.

Probably, though, Walsingham's most valuable and valued agent during this period was Anthony Standen, an English Catholic who had originally left home in 1565 in the service of the ill-starred Lord Darnley and, after a varied career wandering round Europe, had ended up in Florence in the household of the Duke of Tuscany. By the mid 1580s he was also on the strength of the English secret service, using the work name of Pompeo Pellegrini. Relations between Italy and Spain were always close, and Standen was on particularly friendly terms with Giovanni Figliazzi, the Tuscan ambassador to Madrid, who kept him supplied with news and gossip from the Spanish Court as well as acting as his post office when need arose.

In May 1587 Standen told Walsingham that four galleys of the Genoese fleet had been sent to Spain, adding that, since he understood London wanted 'diligence in intelligence of Spanish matters', he had borrowed a hundred crowns and dispatched to Lisbon 'a Fleming who hath there a brother in service with the Marquis of Santa Cruz. . . . I have given him address for his letters to me at the ambassador's house in Madrid who straight will send them to me', continued Standen, adding that he (the Fleming) was 'a proper fellow and writeth well'. Since the Marquis of Santa Cruz was the Spanish Grand Admiral, it seems probable that it was by this means that a copy of a report giving full details of the ships, men and supplies being gathered for the invasion fleet presently came into Walsingham's hands. In the spring of 1588 Standen travelled to Spain himself and reported direct from Madrid and Lisbon.

The great majority of Walsingham's agents, like secret agents in every age, were shadow men, only rarely emerging into the daylight, leaving scarcely a mark on the record. There were one or two exceptions. The great Elizabethan magus, John Dee – alchemist, astronomer, astrologer, mathematician and, some said, wizard – is thought to have assisted the work of the service on an *ad hoc* basis. He would certainly have been able to advise on 'alphabets' or codes, while his extensive travels in eastern Europe offered useful opportunities for intelligence gathering. Then there was the poet and

111

playwright, Christopher Marlowe. There is evidence which seems to indicate that Marlowe was employed on a special mission to France early in 1587, when he was still a student at Cambridge, and again possibly in 1588. His death, stabbed through the eye in a quarrel over the reckoning in Eleanor Bull's tavern in Deptford in May 1593, is held by some to have a sinister connection with his secret past. The presence of Robert Poley, who had played a key role in the breaking of the Babington plot, seems to lend colour to this suggestion. Equally, the cause of the trouble may have been the personal enmity which existed between Marlowe and Ingram Frizer, who struck the fatal blow, later pleading self-defence. We do not know. Like so many happenings on the fringes of the secret world, they keep their secret still.

Francis Walsingham died in April 1590 and most of the European networks died with him. The Queen, relieved since 1588 of her most pressing fears of murder plots and invasion, seemed content to let them go. Even the Principal Secretaryship remained unfilled. Nominal responsibility for the office had passed back to old Lord Burghley, who shouldered the burden on the tacit understanding that his son Robert would soon be taking over. Robert Cecil had been a sickly child with a deformed spine. He had grown into a slender, undersized young man (the Queen called him her pigmy or, in more mellow mood, her elf), but there was nothing undersized about his intellect or his political ambitions.

In the spring of 1591 Elizabeth paid a state visit to Theobalds, the Burghleys' Hertfordshire mansion, staying for ten days at a cost to her hosts of over £1,000. Broad hints were dropped by the family that it would be in everyone's interests if the son of the house were now to receive the Secretaryship; but although the Queen knighted young Robert during her visit and shortly afterwards admitted him to the Privy Council, she did not, contrary to general expectations, make any official appointment. Robert Cecil was still young, still in his twenties, and still learning his trade. The Queen would wait and see how he shaped. But by the end of the year, little Cecil, 'his hands full of papers and head full of matter', had become a familiar sight in the corridors of Whitehall, and it was an open secret that he was already dealing with most of the routine business of the secretariat.

While Robert Cecil enjoyed the undoubted advantage of being his father's son, he was by no means without competitors. By the beginning of the 1590s the scene at Court and Council table was changing as death inexorably removed more and more members of the old guard of Elizabethan public servants – no Elizabethan public servant ever willingly retired from office – and another candidate jostling for royal favour and preferment was another Robert, Robert Devereux, second Earl of Essex.

Nobly born, brilliant and beautiful, Essex was plainly marked out to become a leader of the rising generation and, as such, one whom an ageing sovereign would be wise to keep under her eye and attached to her interests. Apart from this, Elizabeth had a kindness for the boy who possessed some undeniable claims on her generosity. Fatherless from the age of nine (the first Earl having died on royal service in Ireland), young Robert had been one of the Queen's wards. His mother, born Lettice Knollys, was the Queen's cousin, and his stepfather had been the Queen's close friend and constant companion, Robert Dudley, Earl of Leicester.

Essex had made his debut at court in 1584, when he was sixteen, and the following year went with Leicester to the Netherlands to see something of the world and gain some martial experience. He did well in the fighting round Zutphen, where Philip Sidney received his death wound, and Sidney, that beau ideal of Elizabethan youth, had bequeathed his best sword to his 'beloved and much honoured lord, the Earl of Essex'.

When Essex returned to England at the end of 1586 he made an immediate impact on the social scene for, as well as his striking good looks and impressive connections, he was fortunate enough to be endowed with the gift of pleasing, 'a kind of urbanity or innate courtesy', which charmed the Queen and won him a popularity accorded to few other public figures of the time. The Londoners in particular took him to their hearts, gazing with sentimental approval on this 'new adopted son' of royal grace.

Elizabeth was seldom given to sentiment and even more rarely visited by maternal yearnings, but she never lost her eye for an attractive man, and Essex, with his engaging youthfulness, his cozening way and eager devotion, offered a welcome addition to her Court. Soon his tall, red-headed figure was to be seen everywhere at her side, and when her insomnia was troublesome she would keep him with her into the small hours, chatting or playing cards. He was, of course, still far too raw and untried to be trusted with any real responsibility, but he possessed breeding, courage and style, all attributes which the Queen looked for in her young men, and there seemed no reason to doubt that he would go far. Even in those early days, though, he was betraying signs of instability – glimpses of the near psychotic jealousy and touchiness, the all-consuming egotism and uncontrollable temper which were to end by destroying him.

Like any right-thinking young man, the Earl of Essex was set on a military career and incurred serious royal displeasure by running away to join the ill-starred Portugal voyage of 1589. Two years later, however, he succeeded in persuading the Queen to give him command of an expeditionary force intended to assist the new, Protestant, King of France in his struggle against determined Catholic opposition. The expedition was not a success, and by the beginning of 1592 Essex had returned home disenchanted, at least temporarily, with a soldier's life. Instead, he began to consider the possibilities of a career of 'domestical greatness' and thus for the first time, came into direct competition with his near contemporary, Robert Cecil. The two would have known one another as children, when Essex, as a royal ward, had been placed in the charge of Lord Burghley and had spent several months in the great man's household before going up to Cambridge. There is no record of any special relationship – friendly or otherwise – between the boys at that time and since they had grown to manhood their paths had scarcely crossed. Now, though, things were different. Essex was nearly twenty-five and, twice disappointed of military glory, he was ready to try his hand at politics. Unquestionably, he possessed both the brains and talent for public life. When not blinded by paranoia he could put a point of view with eloquence and persuasive charm, besides having the natural leader's flair for drawing men to his side. But in matters of statecraft and high politics he was still an amateur. To be able to challenge such dedicated professionals as Lord Burghley and his son, the Earl needed professional allies, and before the end of 1592 he had found them.

The Elizabethan establishment was very much a family affair, almost all its leading members being connected by blood or marriage or both, and Anthony and Francis Bacon were Lord Burghley's nephews – sons of his wife's sister Ann, who had married the lawyer Nicholas Bacon, Queen Elizabeth's first Lord Keeper. Both brothers possessed trained and brilliant minds; both had been born into the highest political and intellectual circles; both were ambitious, hard-working and astute. It might therefore have been supposed that two such gifted and well-connected young gentlemen would experience no difficulty in carving out honourable and lucrative careers for themselves in the service of the state. But that was not how it had worked out. It seemed there was no place for the Bacons in a world dominated by Lord Burghley, and the brothers had no hesitation in blaming their otherwise inexplicable lack of advancement on the old man's jealousy and determination to reserve all the sweets of office for his son. Simplistic reasoning, and yet the Lord Treasurer's consistent refusal to promote his nephews' cause was surely rooted in some fundamental dislike and distrust. Very possibly, their homosexual proclivities had a good deal to do with it, but old Burghley was a shrewd and experienced judge of men and perhaps he sensed something of the cold-hearted, conscienceless self-seeking which lay beneath the brilliance.

By the early 1590s Francis, now turned thirty and still no more than a back-bench MP practising law at Gray's Inn, had come to the conclusion that it was more than time to seek another patron. He turned to the Earl of Essex and when, in February 1592, Anthony Bacon returned to England after an absence of twelve years spent mostly in the south of France, the younger brother wasted no time in drawing the elder into his new orbit.

Anthony had never been strong and at thirty-three suffered from a painful and often crippling disease described as gout, but which was probably a form of arthritis, a condition not recognized by sixteenth-century medicine. Unlike the more robust Francis, he shrank from the rough and tumble of public life and sedulously avoided the court. Any suggestion that he should pay his duty to the Queen would at once bring on an acute flare-up of his bad leg. Paying his duty to the Earl of Essex was a very different matter. Anthony Bacon had been captivated at first sight by the 'rare perfections and virtues' of this handsome, courteous young nobleman and longed for an opportunity to show the Earl how much he honoured and esteemed his excellent gifts, how earnestly he desired to deserve his good opinion.

The opportunity to serve, in fact, lay ready to hand. During his sojourn in France Anthony had for some time been one of Francis Walsingham's most valued correspondents, passing on information from the agents who slipped to and fro across the Pyrenees and from merchants whose trading vessels plied between the ports of Spain and south-west France. He was also a personal friend and admirer of King Henri IV (who had intervened to save him from the

115

consequences of an unfortunate episode involving page boys) and had acquired numerous French contacts, both Protestant and Catholic.

This, then, was Anthony's chance. While brother Francis acted as Essex's political counsellor, let Anthony take over responsibility for foreign affairs and re-activate the networks which had been allowed to languish since Walsingham's death. His invalidism need be no bar to the work of collecting and collating agents' reports, and there would be no doubt as to the usefulness of the service he would be performing. Detailed, reliable intelligence was always a precious commodity and vital to the successful conduct of affairs. If, with the Bacons' help, the Earl of Essex could begin to acquire the reputation for omniscience which had done so much for Francis Walsingham, it must increase his prestige and give him the right to be regarded as a serious character. For the Bacons, of course, the scheme offered an opportunity not to be missed for undermining the power of the Cecils, and opened up agreeable prospects of being in a position to display their talents independently of Cecil patronage.

Walsingham's agent, Anthony Standen, was an old acquaintance of Anthony Bacon's and sent him regular reports on the state of Spanish affairs during the summer of 1592. Philip, it seemed, was planning an attack on the coast of Brittany, 'from which place the tempest must come towards England' and it would therefore be wise to have a watchful eye on the islands of Guernsey and Jersey. Standen returned to England the following June after an absence of nearly thirty years and, disappointed by the lukewarm welcome he received from Lord Burghley, transferred his allegiance to the Earl of Essex. Another recruit to the new secret service was Antonio Perez, a one time secretary to the King of Spain who had defected to England and sought the protection of Essex House. Perez was a flashy individual, indiscreet and unreliable, but he was amusing company and made himself popular with the Essex House set by his freely expressed dislike of Robert Cecil – 'Roberto il diavolo'. The Earl believed him to be a valuable acquisition, and it was probably through Perez that he was able to score his one notable success in the intelligence field, his victim being the unlucky Dr Ruy Lopez.

Ruy or Rodrigo Lopez, a Portuguese Jew converted to Protestant Christianity, had been settled in London since 1559 and by the mid-1580s was established as a successful and fashionable physician, who numbered Francis Walsingham, the Earl of Leicester, the

Earl of Essex and even the Queen herself among his patients. The origins of his career as a secret agent are obscure, but circumstances point to the arrival in England of Don Antonio, pretender to the throne of Portugal driven into exile by Spain, and his numerous Portuguese retinue – several of whom Walsingham had strongly and quite correctly suspected of being Spanish spies. The Portuguese doctor would have been an obvious choice of instrument to penetrate the activities of his compatriots, and in April 1587 one Antonio de Vega was writing to inform Bernardino de Mendoza in Paris that he had gained over Dr Ruy Lopez 'with good promises' and converted him to King Philip's service.

De Vega went on to hint that Dr Lopez would be prepared to dispose of Don Antonio, by poison if necessary; but Mendoza was sceptical, the doctor reluctant to proceed without written authority, and so the matter rested. By 1590, however, Lopez had become heavily involved in the murky and dangerous world of spy and counter-spy. Manuel de Andrada, code-named David and one of the most efficient and energetic of Philip's agents, reported to Mendoza that, if he received His Majesty's order, Lopez was ready to help negotiate an arrangement with Spain, and that now was the time. He (Lopez) was confident that the Queen would concede any terms demanded of her, as she was in great alarm. If Andrada were given a passport enabling him to go to and fro (and Lopez had undertaken to see to this), then he could come secretly to London, where Secretary Walsingham would speak to him. Lopez hoped that everything might be speedily settled to the King's satisfaction, but in any case, provided the secret was kept, he promised to continue to pass on the decisions taken by the Queen's Council and 'everything that happens of interest to his Majesty'. 'In very truth', Andrada concluded impressively, 'no person can report so well as he can, in consequence of his great influence with the Queen and council.'

There seems little reason to doubt that Lopez was acting under instructions – the putting out of 'peace feelers' being a recognized method of keeping one's adversary off-balance, while at the same time finding out more about his current intentions and strength. It was, of course, a method recognized by both sides, and after speeding 'David' on his way to Madrid, Mendoza recommended that he should be sent backwards and forwards to England under cover of the negotiation, 'so that he may be able to report what is going on there.' But by the time Andrada returned from his mission in the summer of 1591, Walsingham was dead and Lord Burghley seemed unconvinced of his value as a double agent. After some fairly strenuous debriefing, he was released into the custody of Dr Lopez, and after about eighteen months went abroad again to gather news 'in the interests of England'; but he became very dissatisfied with Burghley's niggardly rate of pay and threatened to take his services elsewhere.

Meanwhile, Lopez continued to be employed by the Cecils to monitor the various rather nebulous intrigues being hatched among the Portuguese expatriates in England and the Spanish vice-regal court at Brussels. Exactly why and when he first incurred the ill-will of the Earl of Essex is not clear, although one account says he was unwise enough to gossip with Antonio Perez about certain discreditable details of his noble patient's physique – a breach of professional etiquette which was promptly reported back. Another, more likely explanation is that Essex had got wind of the doctor's connection with Andrada's trip to Spain – again possibly from Perez – and therefore began to regard him with suspicion. Messages passing between members of the Portuguese community and incoming letters containing mysterious references to the price of pearls and the proposed purchase of 'a little musk and amber' were intercepted by Essex House, and in January 1594 Lopez was arrested and taken before Lord Burghley, Sir Robert Cecil and the Earl of Essex.

The doctor vehemently protested his innocence and a search of his house in Holborn revealed nothing incriminating. The result, as Anthony Standen reported to Anthony Bacon, was that when Essex came to court a day or so later, the Queen turned on him, calling him 'a rash and temerarious youth' for making unfounded accusations against a poor man whose innocence she knew well enough. Malice and nothing else lay behind the attack on Dr Lopez and she was particularly displeased because her honour was involved in the matter. But if, as seems probable, Elizabeth was hoping by a display of royal authority to scotch the scandal at birth and save a useful servant and friend, she had miscalculated badly. Uncontrollably furious at such a rebuke, delivered in the presence of Robert Cecil and the Lord Admiral, Essex slammed out of her presence and shut himself up in his private cabinet, refusing to emerge until 'atonement' had been made. The Admiral had to go to and fro smoothing things over, while the Earl flung himself into renewed interrogation of the prisoners (two other Portuguese were also in custody) and a fresh examination of the documents, scarcely pausing for food or sleep until he was satisfied that he had a convincing case. On 26 January he scribbled a triumphant note to Anthony Bacon: 'I have discovered a most dangerous and desperate treason. The point of conspiracy was her Majesty's death. The executioner should have been Dr Lopez: the manner poison. This I have so followed, as I will make it appear as clear as noon day.'

Whether or not Dr Lopez had ever crossed the debatable land separating counter-espionage from treason has long been a matter of purely academic interest; but the only evidence that he was 'deeply touched' in a murder plot consisted of 'confessions' wrung from exhausted and terrified prisoners, ready to admit anything they thought would please. The one fact which did appear as clear as day, though, was that, once the word poison had been mentioned in connection with the Queen, the doctor's doom was sealed. Neither Elizabeth nor the Cecils were prepared to risk a confrontation with Essex over such an emotive issue. Lopez was tried and condemned on 28 February in an atmosphere of intense popular excitement, and although there is some evidence to suggest that the Queen made an eleventh-hour attempt to rescue him (she did ensure that his widow was provided for), he was executed at Tyburn amid the joyful execrations of the mob.

To the general public Lopez the Jew was yet another in a long line of would-be assassins threatening the Queen's precious life, and his unmasking, while it provoked a wave of vicious anti-Semitism, was soon forgotten in the more pressing concerns of the day. To the Queen herself, to Lord Burghley and Robert Cecil the affair had worrying implications, for it had provided a disagreeable illustration of the sort of power Essex and his faction were now able to exert.

It was generally accepted by this time that all matters of intelligence were wholly in the hands of the Earl of Essex and his unofficial spymaster, Anthony Bacon. Anthony, now established at Essex House with his own private office, was receiving regular reports from agents in France, Italy and Spain. He and Essex were also in contact with several correspondents in Scotland, the most valued of whom was a Dr Morrison who was rewarded with money – thirty pounds on one occasion, another time a hundred French crowns plus gifts of stockings and beaver fur hats – for sending intelligence from the Scottish court. Despite the pretensions of fringe candidates such as Arbella Stuart, daughter of Charles Stuart, brother of the murdered Darnley, or of King Philip's daughter, the Infanta Isabella, who, through her father, could boast descent from John of Gaunt and whose claims had recently been canvassed in a work provocatively entitled *A Conference about the next Succession to the Crown of England*, printed in Antwerp under the name of R. Doleman, a pseudonym only thinly concealing the identity of Father Robert Parsons, no one who knew anything of matter had any doubt that King James of Scotland would presently succeed to Queen Elizabeth's throne.

The intentions, inclinations and general well-being of Mary Stewart's son, now in his mid-thirties, a married man with a young son of his own, were therefore of close interest to the political *cognoscenti*. Just how close and detailed that interest was can be judged by the instructions drafted for Morrison by the Essex House staff probably in December 1593, calling for an account of how the King of Scots, referred to as le Chevalier,

> continues, increases or abates of his zeal for the reformed religion. . . . What favour or disfavour he shews to the catholics, especially those of the nobility either publicly or privately; and how he bears the priests, jesuits and dispensers of the papal or Spanish favours among his people. What intelligence or intrigue any of his subjects carry on with either of those two powers with or against his consent, and in what manner he looks upon such subjects.

Morrison was also required to discover what intelligence there was between James and the French King, the Princes of Germany or the states of the Low Countries. Nearer to home, what was James's attitude towards the Queen? Which of her actions pleased him and which did he complain of? What intelligence did he have with her subjects, within or without her kingdoms? What practices were he or any of his subjects, with or without his knowledge, carrying on with the Irish? What faction was there among the Scots with relation to religion, the state, or other private 'causes of contest'? Who were the principal heads or partisans of such factions, and who among them were most favoured or discountenanced by the King?

By the middle of the 1590s the foreign correspondence being conducted under the supervision of Anthony Bacon had become so extensive that the Earl of Essex was having to employ four full-time secretary/linguists. The Queen was ready enough to take advantage of this extra-mural information service and, as the Bacons had calculated, Essex's position as unofficial (and unpaid) Foreign Secretary was giving him useful additional status. Unfortunately, though, the Bacons themselves were not profiting as they had hoped. Anthony seems to have been content to remain in the background, but Francis was ambitious for office. Essex did his best, nagging the Queen to bestow first the vacant Attorney Generalship and then the Solicitorship on the younger Bacon. But although Francis was recognized as a man of wit and learning and a clever lawyer, Elizabeth refused to consider him even for the Solicitor Generalship. It was, in fact, becoming plain that, while Essex could still get almost anything for himself, he could get nothing for his friends, however deserving. The Queen was by now fully aware that the task of containing the Earl within reasonable bounds was going to become more and more difficult. If once she allowed him to start packing her service with his nominees, it might well become impossible. Long experienced in the ways of men, she harboured no illusions about the true worth of Essex's much-vaunted devotion, or about the sort of threat he could come to represent in the hands of abler, more subtle and unscrupulous operators than himself.

In the spring of 1596 Essex abandoned, at least temporarily, his quest for 'domestical greatness', and on 3 June he sailed as joint commander-in-chief of a large and exceptionally well-equipped fleet which had orders to destroy warships and stores in Spanish ports, capture and destroy Spanish coastal towns and seize whatever booty and prizes they could. After a long run of failures and disappointments, everything seemed to favour this latest attempt to singe the King of Spain's beard. The weather was fine, the wind blew fair from the north-east and for once security was good, so that when the English were sighted off the Bay of Cales, or Cadiz, early in the morning of 20 June, surprise was complete.

In the attack which followed, two of Philip's capital warships were captured and two destroyed with appalling loss of life among their crews. 'If any man had a desire to see hell itself, it was there most lively figured', commented Walter Raleigh. The town of Cadiz itself, 'the pearl of Andalusia', was ransacked and burnt, but in the general stampede for glory and loot the English commanders failed to seize merchant shipping valued at 12 million ducats trapped in the inner harbour at Puerto Real in time to prevent the Spaniards themselves from setting fire to it.

When the first reports of the victory reached London, the Queen was generous in her praise and the acclamation echoed round Europe. The taking of Cadiz had been another humiliation for the King of Spain, another brilliant demonstration of English audacity and naval power, and the island's international prestige was back where it had stood in the autumn of Armada year. 'Great is the Queen of England!' they were exclaiming in Venice. 'Oh, what a woman, if she were only a Christian!' At home, the news came as a much-needed tonic for a war-weary nation, and the Londoners had no hesitation in ascribing the credit to their favourite, the Earl of Essex. A sermon preached at St Paul's Cathedral extolling his lordship's 'worthy fame, his justice, wisdom, valour and noble carriage in the action' was received with sustained applause by the congregation and that summer of 1596 saw my lord of Essex reach the zenith of his remarkable career. Hailed as the English Scipio, he had become a popular hero such as even Francis Drake had never been – a cult figure surrounded by an adoring entourage, his every public appearance drawing an eager, jostling crowd of admirers. Internationally, his reputation stood almost, if not quite, as high as the Queen's own. The King of France addressed him as 'Cousin' and foreign diplomats were careful to pay as much respect to Essex House as to Lord Burghley himself. Behind the scenes, however, there was tension.

Elizabeth had not been pleased to hear that the shipping at Puerto Real had been given time to destroy its valuable cargoes, and annoyance turned to rage when it was realized just how much of the booty from Cadiz had found its way into unauthorized hands. The government fought long and hard to separate the returning army from its ill-gotten gains, but without any very noticeable success, and it was being whispered at court 'that the Queen should not hereafter be troubled with beggars, all were become so rich at Cadiz.'

Both commanders-in-chief came in for a share of royal displeasure. When the Lord Admiral Howard of Effingham had the gall to ask for more money to pay the wages of soldiers and mariners already weighted down with plunder which should have gone into the Exchequer, he received a royal rocket. But Her

Majesty's particular wrath seems to have been reserved for the Earl of Essex. Financial grievances apart, Elizabeth's temper had not been improved by the extent of popular acclaim which Essex was currently receiving. She was angry, too, over the large number of knighthoods he had conferred during the expedition. An Essex knight would become an Essex man and, in the Queen's opinion, his lordship's military clientele was already more than large enough for comfort.

Similar misgivings occurred to Francis Bacon, who had held a watching brief on the political scene during his patron's absence and had not failed to note the significance of Robert Cecil's long-delayed appointment to the Principal Secretaryship – made as soon as Essex was safely on his way to Cadiz. Bacon was worried and urged Essex very seriously to play down his popular reputation and his 'military dependence'. What more dangerous image than this could be represented to any monarch living, especially so to a lady and one of Her Majesty's well-known nervous apprehension and dislike of war? But unhappily for all concerned, even if he had been constitutionally capable of following Bacon's wise advice about appearing more amenable to Her Majesty's wishes, taking more trouble to please her in little ways and, above all, trying to remove the impression that he was 'of a nature not to be ruled', Essex was now the prisoner of his military reputation. After Cadiz he became irrevocably type-cast as the country's leading general, and there was to be more work for him that autumn.

The King of Spain, roused from the lethargy of old age and mortal sickness by the disgrace of seeing one of his principal ports fall so easily into the enemy's hands, was hustling his reluctant admirals into an immediate counter-attack. On 10 October the Venetian ambassador in Madrid reported that great preparations were going on in Lisbon. A fleet of some ninety-odd miscellaneous craft had been assembled, of which, according to the Venetians, no more than a third would be fit to fight. Intelligence reports reaching Anthony Bacon from Anthony Rolston, his agent at Fuenterrabia, and letters from an unnamed spy entrenched in the Escorial itself had already given warning that Spain was on the move, and towards the end of October the crews of some captured Portuguese caravels confirmed that the Armada had sailed for an unknown destination commonly believed to be either Ireland or England. The Queen at once turned to the Earl of Essex to organize a Council of War and the whole of the south of England was put on general alert. The militia was mobilized, strategic points along the coast reinforced and contingency plans for a scorched-earth policy were drawn up in case of an enemy landing. The navy was laid up in harbour for refitting after its summer service, but five vessels were hastily commissioned ready to guard the south-western approaches and at the beginning of November orders were issued for the provisioning of another sixteen. The alarm lasted about a month but no more was heard of the Spanish fleet. Not until Christmas did reliable news come in that it had been scattered by a storm off Cape Finisterre and driven back on to its own coasts with heavy losses.

The following summer Essex was off again to Spanish waters but this time there would be no victory, no plunder, no triumphant return. The so-called Islands Voyage ended in disappointment and recrimination and from now on it was downhill all the way. Essex was still a popular favourite, especially with the Londoners, and still commanded a substantial following at Court, where two distinct and hostile factions were beginning to emerge. On the one hand stood Essex and most of the younger, more hot-headed (and impecunious) element, all impatient for the glory and profit to be gained from military adventure overseas. The fact that experience showed glory and profit to be the exception rather than the rule, needless to say, did not for a moment dampen their ardour and they looked on the Earl of Essex as their natural leader. On the other hand was the party of sobersides, favouring a negotiated peace with Spain and led, equally naturally, by Robert Cecil.

The Queen did what she could to keep a balance. She was undoubtedly fond of Essex and had tried long and patiently to tame her 'wild horse'. But although the Earl could still, when he chose, be charming company, such moments were becoming rare. His temper and his paranoia were growing more and more uncontrollable – there were several ugly scenes in the months following the Islands Voyage – and Elizabeth's patience was wearing steadily thinner. Nevertheless, when in 1599 it became urgently necessary to send an army to deal with crisis in Ireland, the Queen seemed to have no option but to appoint Essex as her Lord Lieutenant.

It was, of course, a disaster. After six wasted months floundering through the Irish bogs, culminating in an ill-advised and unauthorized private meeting with the Irish rebel leader, the Earl of Tyrone, Essex abandoned his command and came rushing headlong home to explain to the Queen how impossible it all was. This was the occasion of the famous confrontation at Nonesuch, when my lord of Essex, still spattered with dirt and mire from his journey, burst into the royal bedchamber to find her Majesty 'newly up, the hair about her face'. News of the Earl's approach had, in fact, preceded him by about a quarter of an hour, but it had not reached the Queen and consequently she had no means of knowing whether or not he had brought his army with him, whether the palace might already be in his hands and a *coup d'état* in progress. It was a nasty moment, not made any easier by the fact that she had been caught at a disadvantage, half-dressed and without her wig, but Elizabeth showed no signs of discomposure. Smiling kindly on the unwelcome visitor kneeling at her feet and kissing her hands, she spoke to him soothingly and got rid of him as soon as she could by suggesting he should get washed and changed before they talked again.

Once she realized that Essex had, in effect, simply run away from his responsibilities, apparently relying on her indulgence, or her dependence, to save him from retribution for his gross mismanagement of her affairs and betrayal of her trust, the Queen's mood changed. She became, in fact, justifiably and bitterly angry, but the situation remained tense. Essex still had a number of powerful friends and the danger that the army in Ireland might yet be employed as an instrument of coercion at home could not be disregarded. There was, indeed, a scheme under discussion by certain members of the inner circle of the Essex set – the Earl of Southampton, Christopher Blount, who had married Essex's widowed mother, and Christopher's brother Charles, Lord Mountjoy, lover of the Earl's fascinating sister Penelope Rich – to approach the King of Scots for help; the idea being that James should march an army to the border, where he would demand to be officially recognized as Elizabeth's heir. Mountjoy, nominated as Essex's successor in Ireland, would bring over a contingent of 4,000 or 5,000 men and, together with the Scots, support 'the party that my lord of Essex would make head withal' in a show of force strong enough to compel Elizabeth to name James as her heir, restore Essex to favour and dismiss Robert Cecil. Fortunately for all concerned, James proved too cautious to commit himself and Mountjoy in Ireland wisely had second thoughts, especially as Essex appeared to be in no immediate danger of his life.

The secret was on the whole well kept, but Robert Cecil's spies had been shadowing the messengers to and from the north and he and the Queen knew something and were no doubt able to guess a good deal more about the activities of the Essex party in Scotland and elsewhere. In spite of this, Essex was not committed to the Tower. On the contrary, after a period of house arrest in the custody of Lord Keeper Egerton, he had been allowed to return to Essex House, empty now and stripped of its paraphernalia of power. The busy staff of clerks and secretaries, the secret agents coming and going on their mysterious errands for Anthony Bacon, the jostling queues of petitioners and place-seekers, the visiting dignitaries, the courtiers and captains and hangers-on who had once filled it with bustle and the illusion of power and greatness had vanished. Presently they were replaced by a varied assortment of friends old and new ranging from wild young bucks like the Earls of Rutland and Southampton to militant young Catholics like Robert Catesby and Francis Tresham; from veterans of Essex campaigns like Sir John Davies, Sir Charles Danvers and the Governor of Plymouth, Sir Ferdinando Gorges, to the Earl's secretary, Greek scholar Henry Cuffe, and included a rabble of impoverished lords and gentlemen – all, for one reason or another, losers in the harshly competitive Elizabethan world. Pushing in behind came the bully boys and hoodlums, the discharged soldiers and unemployed captains, the petty criminals and professional trouble-seekers – 'swordsmen, bold confident fellows, men of broken fortunes, discontented persons, and such as saucily used their tongues in railing against all men'.

In the months which had passed since his return from Ireland Essex had used all his wiles to re-ingratiate himself with the Queen, but all to no avail. John Harington, Elizabeth's 'merry godson' who had been with the Earl in Ireland, ventured to visit him in the autumn of 1600 and found him in bitter mood, talking so wildly 'as well proveth him devoid of good reason and right mind.' This may or may not have been the occasion of the venomous remark always attributed to Essex that the Queen's mind had become as crooked as her carcass, but certainly it was clear that he had now given up all hope of recovering his fortunes by fair means and that he and his friends were bent on mischief. Meetings were being held at Drury House, town residence of the Earl of Southampton, and detailed plans made for seizing the Court. Charles Danvers would occupy the Great Chamber and Presence Chamber, John Davies would take the Hall and Christopher Blount the outer gate. When all was ready, Essex, escorted by 'the noblemen of his party', would arrive, force his way into the private apartments and demand the removal of 'such persons as he called his enemies', that is Robert Cecil, Walter Raleigh and Lord Cobham, from about the Queen and their replacement by his own nominees.

The so-called Essex rebellion is sometimes dismissed as no more than the crack-brained folly of a desperate man, half-crazed with disappointment and also, incidentally, up to his eyeballs in debt. But the authorities at the time were not disposed to take the matter lightly. Whitehall Palace was a rambling rabbit warren of a place, virtually impossible to secure. It would be highly vulnerable to surprise attack and there were some violent and determined characters in the mob not gathered a bare twenty minutes away. If they once got into the precincts of the palace no one could say with any certainty whether all the courtiers would remain loyal; nor was it entirely certain how the city would react. Essex, after all, was still Essex, the darling of the Londoners, the hero of Cadiz.

The Queen and Robert Cecil watched and waited. Cecil had a number of spies in Essex House and was keeping a close eye on the comings and goings around the Strand and Charing Cross. Exactly how much he and the Queen knew at this stage about Essex's correspondence with James and the plans for a joint military take-over by the army in Ireland and an invasion force led by the King of Scots remains covered in a good deal of probably deliberate confusion, but by the beginning of February 1601 it was decided that the situation was too dangerous to be allowed to continue and on Saturday 7 February Essex was ordered to appear before the Council to give an account of himself. He refused. He was not well, he said, and in any case he had been warned that the summons was a trap and Walter Raleigh and Lord Cobham were planning to murder him.

At ten o'clock next morning a deputation headed by the Lord Keeper and the Lord Chief Justice arrived at the gates of Essex House demanding admission in the Queen's name, only to be insulted and threatened by the jostling, jeering, cat-calling mob filling the courtyard. It was many years since London had seen such a riotous assembly and the Queen's representatives were rudely seized and locked up in a back room, while Essex and about 200 of

127

his followers attempted to raise the city, running armed through the Sunday streets crying hysterically that a plot was laid for his life and England was sold to the Spaniard. The people came out to stare in amazement at the extraordinary sight of the great Earl of Essex as he rushed sweating and sobbing past their doors but that was all they did. Essex had failed totally and ignominiously to gain support or even credulity for his 'cause'. He retreated to Essex House to find that his hostages had been released and that now, stranded in the ruins of his lurid fantasy world, nothing remained but to bar his doors, burn his papers and prepare to sell his life dearly. In the end, though, there was not even a heroic last stand. Soon after ten that night Essex and Southampton had surrendered to a force commanded by the Lord Admiral, and the Queen, who had sworn not to sleep until she knew they had been taken, was able to go to bed. The 'rebellion' had lasted exactly twelve hours.

The rest of the story is soon told. Essex and Southampton were arraigned together at Westminster Hall on 19 February, charged with conspiring to deprive and depose the Queen's Majesty from her royal state and dignity and subvert the government of the realm; with having refused to disperse their disorderly company and issuing into the city of London with a number of armed men with intent to persuade the citizens to join with them. Both the accused pleaded not guilty and defended themselves boldly, but the trial, like all treason trials of the period, was little more than a formal exercise, notable chiefly for the reappearance of the agile Francis Bacon among counsel for the prosecution.

From Robert Cecil's point of view, everything had turned out very satisfactorily. He had had an opportunity during the course of the trial to force Essex publicly to withdraw the often-repeated slander that Cecil had plotted to sell England to the Spaniard by supporting the claim of the Infanta. He felt reasonably certain, too, that he had got to the bottom of the conspiracy – the evidence of Sir John Davies, Christopher Blount, Charles Danvers and Ferdinando Gorges gave a clear picture of the discussions at Drury House and the plot to seize the Queen, and two days after his trial Essex, influenced by his favourite chaplain, had been moved by a desire to purge himself of guilt by telling all. In a long statement he poured out a detailed account of his own and his friends' activities over the past eighteen months; he named names from Lord Mountjoy downwards and confessed himself to be 'the greatest, the most vilest and most unthankfullest traitor that ever was born'. This was very helpful and not only confirmed much that the government already knew or guessed, but added quite a lot of interesting new information. Fortunately, though, the Earl's impetuous outbreak of 8 February had made it possible to suppress the most damaging of these revelations and Cecil could congratulate himself on a very smooth operation, handled without causing embarrassment to such public figures as Mountjoy (who was proving a great success in Ireland) and the King of Scots.

Essex paid the price of treason to the headsman on Ash Wednesday, 25 February 1601, acknowledging 'with thankfulness to God that he was thus justly spewed out of the realm'. A few weeks later four of his fellow conspirators, Christopher Blount, Charles Danvers, Henry Cuffe and his steward Gilly Meyrick, followed him to the block, but these were the only members of his party to suffer the death penalty. Even the Earl of Southampton had his sentence commuted and lived to become an ornament of a Court where he was far more at home. Francis Bacon, too, would reap the harvest of his patient pragmatism in the next reign, but his crippled brother did not survive to share it. Faithful to his former patron to the end, Anthony Bacon died some time that spring in debt and obscurity.

Essex was gone, and with him went the last flicker of the old England in which an overmighty subject could challenge the central power of the state, even the throne itself, and hope to win. Essex was gone, though his memory lingered on and the people mourned their dead hero in sentimental ballads which were heard even around the Court. 'Sweet England's pride is gone', they sang, but they and England and England's Queen were all much better off without him.

CHAPTER SIX

Gunpowder Treason and Plot

—————◆—————

As the new century came in, the Elizabethan era was drawing inexorably to its close. In August 1598 death had removed Lord Burghley, last and greatest of the friends and councillors who had supported the Queen through all the crises and triumphs of her reign, and now that Essex too was gone, Robert Cecil was left with no serious rival at the council table.

Little Cecil trips up and down,
He rules both court and crown

ran a popular ditty current in 1601, but despite the bad press he has consistently received from historians dazzled by Essex's spurious glamour and despite the fact that he was not quite the man his father had been, 'little Cecil' served the Queen loyally, watching her back at a time when she would have been especially vulnerable to double-dealing.

One of the first consequences of the disappearance of the Earl of Essex from the political scene was a dramatic improvement in the state of Anglo-Scottish relations. Early in February, an embassy of some forty persons headed by the Earl of Mar and an eminent Scottish lawyer, Mr Edward Bruce, was preparing to set out from Edinburgh with instructions to demand official recognition of James's right to the succession of the English crown and to confer privately with the Earl of Essex as to the best means of enforcing Elizabeth's compliance. In the event, they reached London in March, in nice time to congratulate the Queen on her fortunate escape from the Essex conspiracy. Being sensible men, who could see that Robert Cecil was not, as their master had been led to believe, an enemy of Scotland ruthlessly intriguing to advance the claims of the Spanish Infanta, they asked for a meeting, at which the Secretary of State hastened to assure them of his devotion to the King of Scots, for it was time to be thinking seriously about the future.

Since the death of Mary Queen of Scots, the problem of the English succession, for so long the cause of so much anxiety and dissension, had lost most of its urgency. The exiled Catholic community and its allies might continue to discuss it with feverish intensity among themselves and to canvas the claims of a variety of more or less unlikely candidates, but the great majority of Englishmen had gradually grown accustomed to the idea that Mary's son James, who was after all doubly descended from the first Tudor king, would in due time come to occupy his great-great-grandfather's throne.

James himself was rather less sanguine. Like his mother, he yearned for the reassurance of public, parliamentary recognition of his status and, failing to get it, had like his mother begun to turn to the Catholic powers for support. From 1596 onwards rumours were reaching London that the Scottish king was in touch with various foreign courts, that his agents were buying arms from the Grand Duke of Tuscany and that Spanish gold was being poured into the coffers of the Scottish Catholic party. Certainly, James was doing his best to convince Spain, Venice and Rome that he might, in certain circumstances, be prepared to consider receiving instruction in the Catholic faith, or to send his son abroad to be brought up as a Catholic, and as Essex continued to drop hints that the Cecilian faction was working actively against him, he mounted a vigorous propaganda campaign designed 'to blaw abroad' the superiority of the Stuart title.

In fact, Robert Cecil was about to stake his political career on stage-managing a smooth transference to the Stuart title when the time came, and waited only until the Earl of Essex had been removed from the scene before moving into action. Obviously, the first thing was to win James's confidence and endeavour to undo the damage of years of Essex's mischief making, and Cecil therefore embarked on a correspondence with the King which was intended to establish both a confidential relationship and a strong Cecil influence. It was an exceedingly private correspondence, known at the time to no more than half a dozen persons, and elaborate precautions were taken to keep it that way. A cipher was used to conceal the identities of the principal individuals likely to be mentioned – 10 for Robert Cecil, 24 for the Queen, 30 for James and so on – and the letters themselves were carried by special couriers by a secret route.

Knowing her extreme sensitivity on the subject of her successor, Cecil was particularly anxious that the Queen should not get to hear about his covert dealings with the Scots lest, as he put it, her 'age and orbity, jointed to the jealousy of her sex, might have moved her to think ill of that which helped to preserve her.' There can be no doubt that Elizabeth had long regarded James as the rightful heir – witness her care to safeguard his position at the time of his mother's execution – and she almost certainly had a pretty good idea of what her Secretary was up to, but so long as the matter remained officially 'secret', she was content. She trusted Cecil – in the circumstances, she had to trust him – and he did not betray her. He soon had James eating out of his hand, and once that notoriously canny individual was convinced that he had at last acquired a really influential and reliable friend at the English Court, his flirtations with the Catholic powers stopped abruptly. He also stopped pestering for recognition, assuring Cecil that henceforward he would be content to wait for God's good time, rather than hazard the breaking of his neck 'by climbing of hedges and ditches for pulling of unripe fruit.' The fact that 'little Cecil' received cheering promises of favours to come, 'quhen it shall please God that the king shall succiede to his richt', did nothing to alter the other fact that his tactful management of James protected Elizabeth's last years from unnecessary alarms and ensured a peaceful hand-over to the new branch of the family business.

When, in March 1603, it did at last please God that King James should 'succiede to his richt', dissenters on both sides of the great religious divide were hoping for better things. The radical Protestants, or Puritans, could reasonably feel optimistic about a monarch reared from infancy in the Presbyterian Church of Scotland, one of the 'best reformed' churches in Europe, while the Catholics, long fed on rumours of James's Roman leanings, looked forward to receiving at least a measure of toleration and some relaxation of the penal laws. As hostile pressure from abroad had increased and the missionary priests had succeeded in blowing new life into the dying embers of native Catholicism, so the Protestant state had sought to protect itself by enacting ever more repressive legislation directed against the Catholic minority. The fine for recusancy, or non-attendance at the state church, rose from 12 pence to a staggering £20 a month, while attendance at Mass could mean a prison sentence as well as a fine. In 1581 it became a treasonable offence to seek to withdraw any of the Queen's subjects from their natural obedience by reconciling them to the Roman faith. In 1584 all priests, both Jesuit and secular, were ordered to leave the country within forty days. Those who remained, or any others who subsequently attempted to come in, would be adjudged guilty of treason, and any person harbouring such a priest would be guilty of felony. Catholic parents were forbidden to send their children to be educated abroad or to educate them as Catholics at home, and in 1593 the so-called Five Mile Act restricted all obstinate recusants to a 5-mile radius of their homes.

In spite of everything, though, a small, stubborn nucleus of Catholicism had survived and the priests continued to come ashore on moonless nights at some deserted cove or inlet, mostly along the south and east coasts. According to a government proclamation of 1591, they came in a variety of disguises:

> Some in apparell as soldiers, mariners, or merchants. . . . Some come in as gentlemen with contrary names, in comely apparel, as though they had travailed into foreign countries for knowledge . . . and many of them in their behaviour as ruffians, far off to be thought, or suspected to be friars, priests, Jesuits or popish scholars.

Although Robert Parsons had for a time organized an 'underground railway' from a house in Rouen, working in conjunction with William Allen at the college at Rheims, there seems to have been no overall planning authority co-ordinating the missionary traffic. There was, however, plenty of individual initiative shown by the priests themselves, backed up by a network of helpful merchants, inn-keepers, sea-captains and fishermen. A report reaching London in 1602 spoke of a French or, more likely, Flemish merchant called Hermooke, who arranged many secret 'passages' from Calais and Boulogne in fishing boats and other small craft which were able to ply to and fro across the Channel largely unsuspected and unquestioned.

> By these small boats the Jesuits commonly pass in and out . . .
> with all speed and safety. . . . They also use much the help of one
> Gibels, resident in Calais, who with a few hours warning can
> provide at any time a 'schife' or fisher-boat for a sudden passage,
> landing at some odd creek either upon the coast or in the river of
> Thames by night.

It was, as usual, the Jesuits who got all the publicity, although, in
fact, they were very much in the minority. Out of the several
hundred missionary priests at work on the English harvest, the
number of Jesuit fathers in the country at any one time during the
1580s could have been counted on the fingers of one hand. In 1586,
however, the Society's dwindling presence received a vital
reinforcement with the arrival of Fathers Garnet and Southwell.
Like Parsons and Campion before them, Garnet and Southwell
formed a powerful combination of talent. Robert Southwell, the
poet, had all Campion's charm, his other-worldly sweetness of
nature and readiness for martyrdom, though he managed to evade
capture for six years and was not executed until 1594. Henry
Garnet, a Derbyshire man, whose special interests were music and
mathematics, proved even more slippery and resourceful than
Parsons had been and survived for a record period of twenty years.
Like Parsons, he operated a secret printing press and, like Parsons,
organized an efficient system for meeting and helping new priests
coming over from France and Flanders, before posting them to
districts where they were most needed.

Another Jesuit, who arrived in the crisis year of 1588 and who
might, in some respects, be described as the James Bond of the
missionary priests, was John Gerard. Gerard, landing on the
Norfolk coast with three companions one wet November night,
made effective use of his knowledge of the technical terms of
hunting and falconry as a cover – especially when in the company of
those Protestant gentlemen 'who had practically no other conversation.' He proved an exceptionally tough and enterprising
campaigner, but was eventually captured as a result of information
received. Taken to the Tower, he was tortured by 'the manacles' –
that is, hung up by the wrists – in an attempt to get him to betray
Garnet's whereabouts among other things, and Gerard, in his
autobiography, has left a detailed description both of the mechanics
of this particular form of persuasion and of what it felt like.

All the blood in my body seemed to rush up into my arms and hands and I thought that blood was oozing out from the ends of my fingers and the pores of my skin. But it was only a sensation caused by my flesh swelling above the irons holding them. The pain was so intense that I thought I could not possibly endure it.

He did, though, more than once, without uttering a syllable his gaolers wanted to hear. But Gerard was an exceptional case (he subsequently achieved the rare distinction of escaping from the Tower and remained at large until 1606, when he was smuggled out of the country by the Spanish ambassador), and a considerable amount of useful information was obtained from prisoners under torture. In fact, the twentieth century has very little to teach the sixteenth when it comes to the techniques of breaking down a prisoner's resistance. As Robert Southwell wrote:

Some, besides their tortures, have been forced to lie continually booted and clothed many weeks together, pined in their diet, consumed with vermin, and almost stifled with stench. Some have been watched and kept from sleep till they were past the use of reason, and then examined upon the advantage, when they could scarcely give account of their own names.

Apart from the rack, which could dislocate the victim's joints by stretching him between wooden rollers, and the manacles, the most common forms of physical torture seem to have been 'Little Ease', a dungeon so constructed that its inmate could neither stand nor lie, and 'The Scavenger's Daughter', an iron ring which rolled victims into a ball and so crushed them 'that the blood sprouted out at divers parts of their bodies.' Some, too, as Robert Southwell delicately put it, 'have been tortured in such parts, as is almost a torture to Christian ears to hear it.'

Although torture was a familiar enough weapon in the armoury of most contemporary Christian judicial systems, in 1583 the English government had felt impelled to issue an explanation and justification of its use in the interrogation of captured priests. A *Declaration of Favourable Dealing by Her Majesty's Commissioners for the Examination of Certain Traitors* was probably written by Thomas Norton, one of the commissioners concerned with the examination of Edmund Campion. It pointed out that torture was legal in certain cases and affirmed that it was never applied in matters of conscience, but only to uncover treasonable practices. Nor was it used 'at adventure', but only where there were good reasons for believing that the prisoner was concealing evidence.

The argument as to whether the priests were persecuted because they were Catholics, or tried and executed because they were traitors found guilty by due process of the law is still very much a live issue in some circles. But as front-line combatants in the battle for hearts and minds, the missionaries occupied a special category. The great majority of Queen Elizabeth's Catholic subjects, who kept their heads down and kept out of politics, do not appear to have suffered any worse inconveniences than those which have afflicted religious dissidents in many other societies. Few known recusants escaped the notice of the authorities at some time in their lives, but it was often possible to avoid prosecution by adopting stratagems such as temporarily leaving home – for example, pregnant women would go into hiding to avoid having to present their infants for baptism at the parish church – cultivating local officialdom (church-wardens and even priest-hunters could often be either bribed or overawed), and pleading excuses like ill-health or being 'out of charity' with a neighbour to avoid going to church. The penal laws were by no means universally or rigorously enforced – especially in those areas where the local magnates were sympathetic. In many of the remoter country districts Catholic and Protestant families were able to exist quite comfortably side by side, but the saying 'a Catholic always pays his debts', which became current at this time, was probably due not so much to superior moral rectitude as to the fact that no Catholic, who might at any moment have to depend heavily on the goodwill of neighbours, could afford to make a single unnecessary enemy.

But in 1603 it seemed that the climate might be changing for the better. Already, in the old Queen's last years, as the threat from international Catholicism receded, the pressure had begun to ease a little and now, with the arrival of a new sovereign who had been heard to make large promises regarding religious toleration and who, moreover, was not the subject of a papal interdict, even the most cautious Catholics were talking of a new dawn.

And at first all seemed to be going reasonably well. Thomas Tresham, a leading member of the Catholic community in the Midlands, proclaimed King James at Northampton, praying God to prosper him, while his son-in-law Lord Mounteagle, another Catholic, was among the group of gentlemen who secured the Tower for the King. In July a deputation of Catholics was received at Hampton Court and informed by the Lords of the Council that it was his Majesty's intention to remit all recusancy fines and that the Catholics might continue to enjoy this mark of royal favour for as long as they kept themselves 'upright and civil in all true carriage towards the King and State'. In September an embassy arrived from Spain – the first since Bernardino de Mendoza had been expelled almost twenty years before. Certainly, times were changing, for the embassy of Don Juan de Tassis came to open informal negotiations towards a peace treaty and also, incidentally, to see if anything could be done to improve the lot of the English Catholics. The government wanted that peace treaty and was therefore prepared, at least for the time being, to relax its grip. The results were immediate and startling. Over a hundred priests entered the country during the first few months of the reign. The embassy chapels, for a long time centres of secret worship, were thrown open to all comers and even sermons were publicly preached at open-air pulpits.

It could not go on, of course. Apart from anything else, Protestant public opinion as represented by the House of Commons would never have stood for it, and in February 1604, shortly before his first Parliament assembled at Westminster, the King issued a proclamation denying that he had ever intended to give anyone cause to expect 'that he would make any innovation in matters of religion.' The proclamation went on to command all Jesuits, seminaries and other priests to depart the realm, and in his speech to Parliament in March James assured the members that he could not permit the increase of the Catholic religion without betraying himself and his conscience. While the King was still apparently prepared to grant a limited amount of toleration to 'quiet and well-minded' laymen, this was a clear sign that the honeymoon was over and before the end of the summer a Bill for the due execution of the Elizabethan penal statutes against Jesuits, seminary priests and recusants had received the royal assent. The recusancy fines were to be re-imposed and fresh penalties introduced for any person going abroad, or sending a child abroad, in order to be strengthened in the popish religion. There was, in fact, no immediate government crack-down on the Catholic population – the Spanish peace treaty had not yet been finalized and the King was still talking largely about his reluctance to persecute loyal subjects over matters of conscience

– but it was in a general mood of disappointment and disillusion over promises broken that the Gunpowder Plot was born.

Doubt has always existed – and been freely expressed – regarding the veracity of the official account of this best remembered of all attempts to bring down the established order of things, but it seems to be generally accepted that the idea was first taken up by Robert Catesby, son and heir of William Catesby of Lapworth in Warwickshire, whose lineage is respectfully described as 'ancient, historic and distinguished'. Born in 1573, Robert was a fine figure of a man, more than 6 foot tall, good-looking, an accomplished swordsman and athlete. He is said to have possessed a noble and expressive countenance and a persuasive charm of manner which 'exercised an irresistible influence over the minds of those who associated with him.' He had acquired a reputation for wild and extravagant behaviour while still up at Oxford and was always more or less in debt: 'As he kept company with the best noblemen of the land, so he spent much above his rate, and so wasted also a good part of his living.' One of the noblemen Robert Catesby kept company with had been the Earl of Essex. He had been a conspicuous member of the company assembled at Essex House in February 1601 and was fortunate afterwards to escape with a period of imprisonment and a £3,000 fine.

Robert's father had been reconciled to Catholicism by the first Jesuit mission of Parsons and Campion and his mother was a Throckmorton of Coughton, another leading recusant family, but Robert himself seems to have shown no particular religious zeal until after the death of his father in 1598, when he became a born-again Catholic and a reformed character. According to the Jesuit Father Gerard, 'he left his swearing and excess of play and apparel and all wild company and began to use daily practices of religion instead of them, insomuch that his former companions did marvel to see him so much changed.' After the Essex fiasco his ardour was, if anything, increased and he prepared to devote all his energies to the furtherance of the Catholic cause. With this in view, he summoned his close friend and kinsman, Thomas Winter, to come to London for a conference.

The Winters, or Wintours, came originally from North Wales but had settled at Huddington in Worcestershire some time in the reign of Henry VI and were connected by blood or marriage with nearly all the other Catholic familes who became entangled in the

Gunpowder Plot. Thomas, a younger son born about 1565, had been a mercenary soldier at one stage of his career and saw active service with the Dutch army in Flanders, but in 1600 he had made a pilgrimage to Rome and since then had undertaken several diplomatic missions on behalf of the English Catholics. Described as 'strong and comely and very valiant', he was also an educated and cultured man, speaking three languages and mixing easily in aristocratic Catholic circles both at home and abroad. Thomas Winter held some not very clearly defined position in Lord Mounteagle's household, but he was at home at Huddington in February 1604, when Robert Catesby's message reached him. He found Catesby at his house at Lambeth and with him John Wright of Holderness in Yorkshire, another old friend and Catholic activist and another survivor of the Essex affair.

It was at this meeting that Catesby told Winter how 'he had bethought him of a way at one instant to deliver them from all their bonds and, without any foreign help, to replant again the Catholic religion.' He then proceeded to outline his plan, which was 'to blow up the Parliament House with gunpowder; for' he said, 'in that place they have done us all the mischief, and perchance God hath designed that place for their punishment.' Winter was taken aback, but had to agree that Catesby's plan certainly 'struck at the root', but pointed out that if it failed, which seemed only too probable, the consequences for the Catholics were likely to be disastrous. Catesby retorted that the nature of the disease required 'so sharp a remedy' and asked if they could depend on Winter's support. Winter replied rather huffily that 'in this or what else soever, if Catesby resolved upon it, he would venture his life', but he was still anxious to impress his friend with some sense of the practical difficulties which lay ahead, such as 'want of a proper house, and of one to carry the mine, noise in the working and such like.' Catesby was inclined to brush all this aside: 'Let us give the attempt, and where it faileth pass no further.' Eventually, however, it was agreed that in order to leave 'no peaceable and quiet way untried', Thomas Winter should go over to Brussels and make a last effort to persuade the Spanish negotiatiors, then on their way back to England, to stipulate for some measure of religious toleration to be written into the final draft of the peace treaty. This he did, but got nothing but fair words. Spain wanted peace too badly to do anything which might jeopardize the treaty. From now on the English Catholics were on their own.

Winter was more successful over the other part of his mission – to recruit 'some confident gentleman' from among the English in the Low Countries who would be a useful man in a tight corner – and returned to London towards the end of April 1604, bringing with him Guy Fawkes. Guy, or Guido, Fawkes, the only one of the Gunpowder Plotters whose name is generally remembered, was another Yorkshireman, born in 1570, son of William Fawkes, a notary in the city of York who held the office of Registrar and Advocate of the Consistory Court. A pious Catholic, Guy had opted for a career as a professional soldier in the Spanish Army in the Netherlands, enlisting in the English Regiment under the command of Sir William Stanley. He became a well-known and respected member of the English community in Flanders, and was recommended to Thomas Winter as being 'a fit and resolute man' for the execution of any enterprise. By this time Robert Catesby had added another initiate to the original party. This was Thomas Percy, a poor relation to Henry Percy, ninth Earl of Northumberland, the so-called Wizard Earl, who served him in the capacity of steward. Thomas Percy was something of a crook – at least the Earl's tenants frequently complained that he had swindled them – but he was a known Catholic and apparently eager for action. 'Well, gentlemen, shall we always *talk*, and never *do* anything?' was his cry. His importance to the plot was his connection with a great nobleman and the fact that he held a minor post at Court. He thus became a 'front man' for the rest and at the end of May the lease of a house adjoining the House of Lords was taken in his name. The plan was to dig a tunnel from the cellar of this house, while Catesby's lodging at Lambeth would be used as a temporary store for timber props, tunnelling tools and, of course, gunpowder. It was agreed that Guy Fawkes, whose face would not be known to the government's spies, should pose as Thomas Percy's servant under the name of Johnson. He was handed the keys of the Westminster house and left there as caretaker. A sixth conspirator, Robert Keyes, was installed at Lambeth. Parliament having now been adjourned until February 1605, Catesby and the others dispersed, arranging to meet again at Michaelmas.

What with one thing and another it was the second week of December before serious tunnelling could begin and it quickly turned out to be a harder and slower task than they had expected. It took a fortnight to reach the actual foundations of the Parliament building and they still had to tackle the 11 foot thick foundation wall. Even with extra help – Robert Keyes had been brought over from Lambeth and John Wright's brother Christopher also recruited to the tunnelling party – it was clear they would never be ready by the time Parliament re-assembled. Then came a stroke of luck. Just before Christmas it was announced that the session had been prorogued again until the following October. Tunnelling continued through January and February, but hit another snag when water began to seep into the workings. By about mid-February it had become obvious that no explosive charge could be laid in a tunnel now rapidly filling with water. The original plan must, therefore, be abandoned and Thomas Winter made up his mind to go abroad again. But before the conspirators finally gave up hope and went their separate ways, another stroke of luck transformed the situation. A cellar, or rather a ground-floor store-room, which lay most conveniently just above the flooded tunnel and just below the chamber of the House of Lords suddenly and unexpectedly became vacant. Thomas Percy at once applied for the tenancy on the pretext that he wanted it for his wood and coals and obtained possession on Lady Day, 25 March. Now it only remained to ferry the gunpowder, about twenty barrels, across the river from Lambeth. This was done under cover of darkness; the powder, in large hampers, arranged in its new home together with some large stones, iron bars and other tools used in the tunnelling operations so as to make the explosion, when it came, the more destructive. The whole was then concealed under a load of firewood with a quantity of miscellaneous lumber and empty bottles artistically disposed to complete the deception. By about the first week in May all was ready. The door of the store-room was locked, the conspirators 'having first placed certain marks about the door inside' so that they would know if anyone had broken in during their absence. They then agreed to separate, arranging a rendezvous in London in September.

There is a school of thought which goes so far as to maintain that the Gunpowder Plot was a put-up job from the beginning – brainchild of Robert Cecil, who somehow contrived to plant the idea in Robert Catesby's head. There is, naturally enough, no direct evidence to support such a theory and it seems inherently improbable. Cecil, or the Earl of Salisbury as he had now become, was an

141

exceedingly busy man. As the King's chief minister he carried the burden of all the ordinary cares of state, and in 1604 was also responsible for overseeing the progress of the Spanish peace process and James's controversial plan for an Anglo-Scottish union – both complex and sensitive issues requiring a high level of concentrated attention. Nor, in 1604, did the Catholic problem appear especially pressing. The Catholics had recently lost a good deal of credibility at home by reason of their bitter feuding and, with Spain eager for peace, they were not going to be able to call on foreign aid, at least for the foreseeable future. This, of course, did not mean that the government was not still keeping a close eye on their activities. Francis Walsingham's secret service was still very much in being and the new Lord Salisbury was fast acquiring his predecessor's reputation for omniscience. His principal aides in matters of intelligence were the unlikeable but efficient Sir William Waad, formerly Clerk to the Privy Council and now Lieutenant of the Tower, and the Attorney General Edward Coke, but most of the work of handling the agents and collating their reports was done by Sir Thomas Challoner, a former diplomat with strong Scottish connections.

Some demonstration by Catholic activists disappointed in their expectations of the new reign had been more than half anticipated, so when, as early as April 1604, the 'discoverers' who specialized in watching the movements of known recusants and their friends began to pick up the scent of a possible conspiracy, higher authority was not particularly surprised. But when it appeared that men of the social standing of Robert Catesby, Thomas Winter, Thomas Percy and the Wright brothers were involved, higher authority became very interested indeed.

These first reports came from an agent named Henry Wright (no relation to John and Christopher), a trusted operative who held a minor post at Court, and another shadowy figure, known only as Davies. These were valuable sources as far as they went. They could learn from servants' chatter who had suddenly decided to go on a visit to London, or which gentlemen had recently formed the habit of meeting regularly for supper and private conversation. They could observe such gentlemen crossing the river to Lambeth Stairs, foregathering at the sign of the Duck and Drake off the Strand or making their way unobtrusively to a house in the fields beyond Clements Inn. But they could not hope to overhear what was being discussed behind closed doors and shuttered windows. In order to do that, it would be necessary to penetrate the inner circles of the conspirators by using the time-honoured method of 'putting some Judas amongst them.'

Again, there is no direct evidence that this is what happened in the case of the Gunpowder Plot – such arrangements are not normally committed to paper – but it would certainly offer a plausible explanation for a number of subsequent events, and the government was fortunate in having a well-qualified Judas most conveniently ready to hand. William Parker, Lord Mounteagle, possessed an impeccable Catholic background. His paternal grand-father had gone abroad in the late 1560s to join the religious refugees living under Spanish protection; his mother, daughter and heiress of the third Baron Mounteagle, had been a Stanley, a family well known for its Catholic sympathies, and William himself had married the daughter of Thomas Tresham. An apparently commit-ted Catholic, 'bred up in the Romish religion', he had been another of the rash young men involved in the Essex rebellion and, like his friend Robert Catesby and brother-in-law Francis Tresham, had been lucky to escape with a fine. But unlike Catesby and Tresham, Mounteagle had been taken back into favour by the Protestant establishment, and the suggestion is that he had paid his way by offering to turn into an informer. There is no suggestion that Mounteagle was himself among the Gunpowder conspirators, but he was well known to, and trusted by, them – Thomas Winter was a member of his entourage – and he was in an unrivalled position for picking up useful items of information about the young Catholic activists in his circle. The probability, therefore, that it was Lord Mounteagle who told Lord Salisbury that the Catholic activists with whom he mixed socially were planning to blow up the Parliament House and with it the King and as many of his ministers as possible, is too strong to be lightly disregarded.

Lord Salisbury may not personally have dreamt up the idea of the Gunpower Plot, but nothing could have suited his general political purposes more perfectly. Such an atrocity would not only serve to discredit the Catholic party for a generation and put an end to all loose talk about toleration, but would also, with any luck, bring about the downfall of the Earl of Northumberland, whom Salisbury regarded as a dangerous enemy, and provide further ammunition against the Jesuits. The plotters were therefore worthy of every encouragement and when their tunnelling operations ran into difficulty, a comfortable dry storeroom was thoughtfully provided for their use.

During the summer of 1605 Robert Catesby was busy in his home base of the south Midlands organizing the military operation which would have to be ready poised to follow up the explosion at Westminster. Always supposing this had been successful and the King, his eldest son and Robert Cecil were all dead, the next in succession to the throne would be the five-year-old Prince Charles or nine-year-old Princess Elizabeth. Thomas Percy was given the task of seizing the Prince and carrying him safe away, but Charles was in London and might be inaccessible to kidnappers. The Princess Elizabeth, on the other hand, was living in the charge of Lord Harington at Combe Abbey near Coventry and no more than some 20 miles from Catesby's mother's house at Ashby St Leger and the Winter estate at Huddington. It should be a simple matter to snatch her 'by drawing friends together at a hunting near the Lord Harington's and Ashby, Mr Catesby's house'. What was needed was a troop of cavalry; local gentlemen, their servants and tenants, well armed and mounted, ready and waiting to escort the new Queen to London with the least possible delay.

The plan was not quite as fantastic as it sounds. The atmosphere in the capital in 1605 was very different from that at the time of the Essex fiasco. Catesby intended to make a proclamation showing that but for the bold action of the Gunpowder Plotters, Parliament would have ratified the deeply unpopular union between England and Scotland and hoped that by appealing to rampant anti-Scottish prejudice, he might persuade the Londoners to support his *fait accompli*. First, though, the conspirators would have to widen their circle to include men who possessed the sort of wealth and status necessary for raising an army and if all went well, for forming a government.

With this end in view, John Grant of Norbook near Warwick, another former Essexian, and Thomas Winter's elder brother, Robert, squire of Huddington, had already been enrolled, and later in the summer Sir Everard Digby, Ambrose Rookwood and Francis Tresham were added to the list. These five were admitted to the inner circle of the plot, but various other 'enterprising and discontented gentlemen' approached by Catesby were told only of a plan

144

to raise a new regiment of volunteers to serve under the Archduke of Austria in Flanders.

As autumn drew on the conspirators began to put the final touches to their plan of action, meeting at White Webbs, a house in Essex much used by the Jesuits for conferences and retreats. It was agreed that Guy Fawkes was to be responsible for actually lighting the fuse which would set off the explosion, using a slow burning match so as to give himself a margin of about fifteen minutes to get on board a ship waiting on the Thames to take him to safety in Flanders. There was also some discussion about the desirability of warning certain Catholic peers against attending the opening of Parliament and several names were mentioned, including Lord Mounteagle.

Lord Mounteagle was often to be found at this time mingling quite naturally at social occasions with his old friends Robert Catesby and Tom Winter and his brother-in-law, Francis Tresham, and was still, it is to be presumed, reporting progress to Lord Salisbury, either in person or through the agency of his confidential secretary, Thomas Ward, who is thought to have been a government spy. Lord Salisbury had been making his own final dispositions. He had a list of the conspirators – not quite complete, as it did not include Everard Digby or Francis Tresham. He knew – it would not have been difficult to deduce – that the expected armed rising would come from the Midland counties and had taken the obvious precaution of warning the sheriffs most likely to be affected. All that remained was to arrange to have the plot 'discovered' in a suitably artistic manner.

Parliament had been prorogued once more and the date for the State Opening was now set for Tuesday, 5 November. On Saturday, 26 October Lord Mounteagle suddenly announced his intention of visiting his house at Hoxton on the eastern outskirts of London, and ordered supper to be prepared for him there. At about seven o'clock that evening, as he was about to sit down to his meal, a letter was brought in by one of his pages, who said it had been handed to him by a man in the street outside, a stranger 'whose features he could not distinguish.' The stranger had asked if Lord Mounteagle was at home and, on being told that my lord was then at supper, had handed the boy a letter, 'enjoining him "to deliver it into his master's own hands, as it contained matters of importance." ' His lordship broke the seal and, 'perceiving the same to be of an unknown and somewhat unlegible hand, and without either date or subscription', passed it to his secretary, Thomas Ward, to decipher. The letter, which was addressed 'To the right honorable the lord mowteagle', ran as follows:

> my lord out of the love i beare to some of youer friends i have a caer of youer preservacion therefor i would advyse yowe as yowe tender youer lyf to devyse soem exscuse to shift of youer attendance at this parleament for god and man hathe concurred to punishe the wickednes of this tyme and thinke not slightlye of this advertisment but retyere youre self into youre contri wheare yowe maye expect the event in safti for thowghe theare be no apparence of anni stir yet I saye they shall receyve a terrible blowe this parleament and yet they shall no seie who hurts them this councel is not to be contemned because it maye do yowe good and can do yowe no harme for the dangere is passed as soon as yowe have burnt the letter and i hope god will give yowe the grace to mak good use of it to whose holy proteccion i commend yowe.

Lord Mounteagle, much perplexed and 'notwithstanding the lateness and darkness of the night in that season of the year', went at once to Whitehall to show the mysterious letter to Lord Salisbury and be congratulated on his good sense and judgement. Thus the stage was set for the dramatic searching of the vaults and cellars beneath the Lords' chamber and the discovery of the villainous Guy Fawkes lurking among the barrels of gunpowder, lantern in hand, slow matches and touchwood on his person – a scene which has passed into English folklore along with King Alfred burning the cakes, Francis Drake on Plymouth Hoe and other such never to be forgotten episodes.

The identity of the anonymous letter writer remains a matter of conjecture. The conspirators themselves, who were thoughtfully informed of the progress of events by Thomas Ward, at first believed Francis Tresham to be the culprit and would have killed him had he not been able to convince them of his innocence. Tresham has nevertheless remained the favourite suspect in official Protestant accounts. Catholic historians prefer to regard the letter as a government device and composed, perhaps, by Lord Salisbury himself, and although again there is no direct evidence the probabilities do point in this direction. Certainly, it is hard to credit that Mounteagle, who had been so often in their company and was on such familiar terms with Catesby and the others, did not have an exceedingly good idea of what they were up to, and if Francis Tresham had really wanted to warn his brother-in-law, why should he have gone to so much unnecessary trouble and taken such an unnecessary risk? They were, after all, in frequent contact socially, and a few words muttered in the privacy of the jakes would have been enough. But if Robert Cecil wanted to provide himself with an excuse to 'discover' the treason without revealing his sources – 'I dare boldly say no shower nor storm shall mar our harvest', he had written to a friend on 24 October – then the facts fit the circumstances, even to Mounteagle's sudden decision to spend the night at Hoxton, a house he very seldom visited. There would, it has been pointed out, be less chance of Cecil's messenger being seen and perhaps recognized than if 'the little comedy at Hoxton' had been played in central London. The text of the letter, too, was in its way a little masterpiece – just sufficiently obscure to make it genuinely puzzling to the innocently uninitiated, but not so obscure as to make its unravelling by professionals look unnaturally convenient.

The conspirators, meanwhile, were in a state of considerable nervous agitation and indecision. However, when several days passed without any sign from officialdom, they appear to have convinced themselves that the letter must have been a hoax. They held a final meeting in London on Sunday 3 November and decided to go ahead with the plan to rendezvous in the Midlands.

Events now took their inevitable course. The arrest of Guy Fawkes and the horrifying discovery of 'a treason in which the King and the Lords should have been blown up' put an immediate end to the never very credible chances of a general Catholic uprising. On Friday 8 November Robert Catesby, Thomas Winter, Thomas Percy, the Wright brothers, John Grant and Ambrose Rookwood were surrounded at Holbeach House near Stourbridge by a posse led by the Sheriff of Worcester, and in the subsequent shoot-out Catesby, Percy and the two Wrights were killed, Thomas Winter, Ambrose Rookwood and John Grant wounded.

From the point of view of Robert Cecil and his secret service, the outcome was highly satisfactory. Cecil had even been able to implicate the Earl of Northumberland, for was not Thomas Percy his kinsman and servant who would never have joined the conspiracy without the knowledge and permission of his noble patron and who had actually dined at Syon House on the eve of the intended atrocity.

147

All that was lacking now was evidence to incriminate the dreaded Jesuits, but Cecil had every confidence that this would in due course be forthcoming. On 13 January 1606 one of the lesser conspirators, Thomas Bates, admitted that he had been sent by Catesby to tell Father Garnet, the Jesuit Superior, and Father Tesimond of Guy Fawkes' arrest and to ask for their help in rallying the Catholics. According to Bates, Garnet replied that he marvelled Catesby and the others could contemplate such wicked actions, that he would not meddle and wished them to give over. However, after some discussion, Father Tesimond, also known as Greenway or Greenwell, had accompanied Bates back to Huddington to confer with Catesby. This, it was felt, was more than enough to justify warrants for the arrest of Garnet, Tesimond and John Gerard, who was believed to be in the Midlands and in close contact with the other priests. In the event, Father Tesimond succeeded in escaping to France and Gerard was presently smuggled out of the country in the Spanish ambassador's suite. But Garnet was traced to Hinlip near Worcester, the home of Thomas Abington, another of Lord Mounteagle's brothers-in-law. Hinlip was more than usually well provided with hiding places, and, despite their best endeavours, the searchers failed to find Garnet and his companion Father Oldcorne. Eventually, however, after a siege lasting more than ten days, the two priests were forced to come out of a space too small to stand up in or, sitting, to straighten their legs. Besides which, 'in regard the place was so close those customs of nature which must of necessity be done . . . was exceedingly offensive to the men themselves and did much annoy them that made entrance upon them.'

By a grim coincidence, 27 January, the day Garnet was captured was also the day the surviving conspirators were being tried in Westminster Hall. They were executed in two batches on 30 and 31 January, so that all the witnesses who could have testified at Garnet's trial were dead two weeks before he had even been brought to London. This was, presumably, deliberate policy. Lord Salisbury wanted no possible conflict of evidence, no lingering doubt left in anyone's mind 'that the principal offenders are the seducing Jesuits; men that use the reverence of religion Yea, even the most sacred and blessed name of Jesus as a mantle to cover their impiety, and treason.' Nor doubt that 'the Jesuits were so far engaged in this treason, so that some of them did not stick to say, when they heard it had miscarried that they were utterly undone.'

Serious efforts were made to induce Garnet to admit that he had had prior knowledge of the Gunpowder Treason or, better still, that he had helped to plan it and at last, under torture, he owned to having had 'a simple knowledge', but only under the seal of the confessional. It seems unlikely that the Jesuits had been in any way actively involved in the preplanning. Papal policy was now strongly against any sort of violence, which could only be damaging to the Catholic cause, and in favour of trying to reach some sort of accommodation with King James's government. On the other hand, Garnet and the others were all highly intelligent men, their senses sharpened by constant exposure to danger. They were all well acquainted with the Catholic activists. They lived in their houses, heard their confessions, directed their spiritual lives, tutored their children, mixed with their wives and servants. It is straining credulity to believe they knew nothing of what was going on.

Really, though, it hardly mattered. The important thing, as Lord Salisbury himself made brutally clear, was

> to demonstrate the iniquity of the Catholics, and to prove to all the world that it is not for religion, but for their treasonable teaching and practices, that they should be exterminated. It is expedient to make manifest to the world how far these men's doctrinal practice reacheth into the bowels of treason and do, for ever after, stop the mouths of their calumniation that preach and print of conscience.

This, of course, had been the object so doggedly pursued by Francis Walsingham, by the Cecils, father and son and other loyal servants of the Protestant Crown for the past half century. It had been a bitter struggle and inevitably some ugly things had been done in its name, but its insistence on approaching the matter from a secular angle had undoubtedly helped to save England from the religious wars which ravaged Continental Europe in the sixteenth and seventeenth centuries.

The unmasking of the great Gunpowder Treason marked the effective end of the long and complicated saga of intrigue, plot and counter-plot which had begun with the Ridolfi affair in the 1560s. The full truth of the story of the Great Treason is never likely to be known – too much vital evidence is missing, too much sectarian passion has clouded the issue – but what is certain is who benefitted. Rumours that Lord Mounteagle had been one of the conspirators and had betrayed his friends to Lord Salisbury were vehemently denied – a little too vehemently perhaps – and the Attorney General was instructed to avoid making any definite statement as to the authorship of the notorious anonymous letter in his conduct of the trials. Mounteagle was publicly commended for 'his discretion and fidelity', and 'his loyal and honourable care of his Prince and country' was rewarded with a pension of £700 a year. Salisbury himself was admitted to the Most Noble Order of the Garter, and the Venetian ambassador reported that 'the pomp was such that the like of it is not in the memory of man; indeed all confess that it surpassed the ceremony of the very King's Coronation.' The ambassador considered that Robert Cecil's power would last, for it was based not so much on royal favour 'as on an excellent prudence and ability which secure for him the universal opinion that he is worthy of his great authority and good fortune.' In fact, the breaking of the Gunpowder Plot marked the zenith of Cecil's career. Six years later he was dead, by which time his pre-eminence had begun to decline.

The short-term consequences of the Gunpowder Plot were predictable. The Parliament which finally assembled in January 1606 in an atmosphere of red hot anti-papal fervour reminiscent of the 1580s, immediately declared 5 November a day of public thanksgiving to be observed annually in every cathedral and parish church within the realm of England. The members went on to pass two new penal laws against the native Catholics – an Act for the Better Discovering and Repressing of Popish Recusants, and an Act to Prevent and Avoid Dangers which may Grow by Popish Recusants. The outlook for the embattled English Catholics thus looked as grim as at any time for the past fifty years, but nevertheless better days were coming, and sooner than anyone could have foreseen in 1606. The long-drawn-out and ultimately unsuccessful negotiations intended to provide a Spanish Catholic bride for the King's heir, followed by the arrival in 1625 of a French Catholic Queen Consort naturally helped to ensure at least a measure of toleration. But although Protestants, and especially those of the radical Puritan variety, complained loudly about the general increase of Catholicism at home and the general failure to enforce the penal laws, no one could deny that the threat from international Catholicism had all but disappeared. It was not until the government of the Protectorate began to feel menaced by dissidents at home and exiled royalists abroad that a secret service, on anything like the scale of that operated by Francis Walsingham, began to re-emerge under the able and energetic direction of Cromwell's spy-master, John Thurloe. Once again a network of agents and informants reached into every corner of Europe, from Stockholm to Lisbon, sending regular reports back to London on everything from the dispositions of the Dutch fleet to the sighting of a strange object in the heavens over Prague, or an outbreak of plague in Danzig.

Index

Abington, Edward, 101
—— Thomas, 148
Algiers, 54
Alva, Ferdinand Alvarez de Toledo,
    Duke of, 6, 11, 17, 22, 29,
    30, 31, 32, 34, 35, 39, 40,
    42, 43, 45, 49
Andrada, Manuel de, 117
Angus, Archibald Douglas, Earl of,
    81
Antonio, Don, 117
Antwerp, 2, 23, 26, 120
Arundel, Charles, 107, 108, 109
—— Henry Fitzalan, 12th Earl of,
    11, 13, 38, 41, 46
—— Philip Howard, 13th Earl of,
    57, 106
Aston, Sir Walter, 101

Babington, Anthony, 97, 98, 99,
    100, 101, 102
Bacon, Anthony, 114, 115, 116,
    118, 119, 120, 121, 123,
    126
    death of, 129
—— Francis, 114, 115, 116, 121,
    123, 128, 129
—— Nicholas, 20, 36, 114
Bailly, Charles, 22, 23, 24, 25, 26,
    27
    interrogated by Lord Burghley, 28
    confesses, 29, 30, 35, 39, 41

released from prison, 46
Ballard, John, 96, 97, 98, 100
Banister, Laurence, 36, 37, 38, 46
Barker, William, 38, 39, 40, 46
Barnard, Robert, 105
Barnwell, Robert, 101
Barty, Francis, 23, 41
Basle, 53
Bates, Thomas, 148
Beaton, James, Archbishop of
    Glasgow, 36, 37, 40, 77, 78,
    80, 83, 95
Belgium, 22
Benavides, Peter, 1
Berden, Nicholas see Rogers, Thomas
Berwick, 80
Bickley, Ralph, 107
Blois, Treaty of, 48, 49, 52
Blount, Charles, 8th Lord
    Mountjoy, 125, 128, 129
—— Christopher, 125, 127, 128,
    129
Bodenham, Roger, 61
Boleyn, Mary, 53
Bolton Castle, 10
Bothwell, James Hepburn, 4th Earl
    of, 12, 42
Bowes, Robert, 77
Bray, William, 106
Brinkley, Stephen, 107
Brooke, William see Cobham,
    William Brooke, Lord

—— Thomas, 23, 46
Brown, Thomas, 36, 37
Bruce, Edward, 130
Brussels, 22, 26, 28, 29, 30, 32, 44,
    110, 118, 139
Burghley, Lord, *see* Cecil, William
Burnham, Edward, 110

Cadiz, 110, 121, 122, 123, 127
Campion, Edmund, 67, 68, 69, 70,
    71, 72, 73, 74, 134, 135,
    138
Calvin, John, 49
Camden, William, 4, 13, 55, 97,
    101, 102
Carey, John, 53
Catesby, Robert, 126, 138, 139,
    140, 142, 143, 144, 145,
    146, 147, 148
—— William, 138
Catherine de Medici, 49, 50, 65
Catlyn, Maliverny, 105
Cavalcanti, Guido, 14, 43
Cecil, Robert, 1st Earl of Salisbury,
    113, 114, 116, 118, 119
    appointed Secretary of State, 123,
    124, 125
    and Essex rebellion, 126–9, 130,
    131, 132
    and Gunpowder Plot, 141–8, 149,
    150
—— William, 1st Lord Burghley, 5,
    6, 7, 11, 13, 14, 15, 16, 17,
    19, 21, 22, 23, 24, 25, 26,
    27, 28, 29, 30, 32, 35, 36,
    38, 41, 44, 45, 46, 48, 53,
    54, 62, 63, 67, 89, 112, 114,
    115, 116, 118, 119, 112
    death of 130, 149
Challoner, Sir Thomas, 142
Charles IX, King of France, 49, 50,
    51, 57
Charles, Prince, 144
Charnock, John, 101
Chartley Manor, 92, 93, 94, 98, 99,
    101, 102
Chateauneuf, Baron de, French
    ambassador, 94
Chatsworth, 20, 45
Cobham, Sir Henry, 77

Cobham, Henry Brooke, Lord, 127
—— William Brooke, Lord,
Warden of the Cinque Ports, 23,
    24, 25, 39, 41, 46
Cockyn, Henry, 56, 57
Coke, Edward, 142
Coligny, Admiral, 49, 50, 51, 87
Como, Cardinal of, 19, 90
Constantinople, 54
Corunna, 61
Creighton, William, 78, 80, 88
Cromwell, Thomas, 11
Cuffe, Henry, 126, 129
Curle, Gilbert, 101, 102
Cuthbert, John, 30, 39, 40

Danvers, Sir Charles, 126, 128, 129
Darnley, Henry Stuart, Lord, 8, 9,
    111
Davies, Sir John, 126, 127, 128
Dee, John, 111
Delgado, John, 1
Denny, Sir Antony, 53
Derby, Earl of, 38
Devereux, Robert *see* Essex, Robert-
    Devereux, 2nd Earl of
Digby, Sir Everard, 144, 145
Dingle Bay, 60
Douai, 61, 62, 63
Douglas, Archibald *see* Angus, Earl
    of
—— George, 83
Drake, Sir Francis, 110, 122, 146
Dryland, Christopher, 107
Dublin, 60
Dudley, Robert *see* Leicester,
    Robert-Dudley, Earl of
Dumbarton Castle, 31, 81
Dunne, Henry, 101
—— John, 61

Edinburgh, 4, 9, 49, 76, 78, 83, 130
Edinburgh, Treaty of, 3
Edward VI, King of England, 53
Egerton, Sir Thomas, Lord Keeper,
    126, 127
Elizabeth I, Queen of England, 1
    and Spanish pay-ships, 2
    Mary Queen of Scots and the
    succession, 3–4, 5, 7

Elizabeth I (*continued*)
  considers Mary's future, 8–10, 11
  Norfolk marriage scheme, 12–13,
    14, 15
  excommunicated, 17–18, 20, 21,
    22, 30, 31, 32, 33, 35, 39,
    41, 42, 43, 44, 45
  signs Norfolk's death warrant, 46,
    47, 48, 51, 52, 53, 54, 55,
    56, 57, 58, 59, 61, 63, 66,
    67, 68, 76, 80, 81, 85, 86,
    87
  and Parry Plot, 88–90, 95, 96, 98,
    99, 103, 104, 108, 110, 112
  and Earl of Essex, 113, 115, 117
  and Dr Lopez 118–19, 120, 121,
    122, 123, 124, 125, 126,
    127, 128, 129, 130, 132,
    136
Elizabeth, Princess, 144
Elliot, George, 72, 73, 74
Ely, Bishop of, 31, 40
Emerson, Ralph, 67, 68, 69
England, 1, 3, 6, 10, 12, 14, 18, 19,
    20, 22, 29, 39, 40, 44, 54,
    56, 59, 64, 65, 67, 72, 76,
    78, 79, 80, 81, 82, 83, 86,
    88, 89, 93, 95, 98, 105, 107,
    117, 118, 123, 128, 144, 150
Englefield, Sir Francis, 23,
    26, 30, 41, 95, 102
Erskine, John *see* Mar, John Erskine,
    1st Earl of
Essex, Robert Devereux, 2nd Earl
  of, 92, 113, 114, 115, 116,
    117, 118, 119
  raid on Cadiz, 121–3, 124, 125,
    126, 127
  trial and execution, 128–9, 130,
    131, 138

Fagot, Henry, 84, 85
Fawkes, Guy, 140, 145, 146, 147,
    148
Fawkes, William, 140
Fiesco, Thomas, 14
Figliazzi, Giovanni, 111
Fitzalan, Henry *see* Arundel, 12th
    Earl of
Fitzherbert, Thomas, 107

Fitzmaurice, James, 60
Flanders, 15, 17, 23, 26, 32, 40, 49,
    59, 87, 105, 134, 139, 140,
    145
Florence, 14, 146, 111
Foljambe, Godfrey, 107
Forster, Sir John, 80
Fotheringay Castle, 102
Fowler, William, 84
France, 1, 2, 5, 6, 12, 15, 33, 40,
    47, 48, 51, 52, 53, 54, 55,
    61, 62, 74, 76, 77, 78, 81,
    82, 83, 84, 89, 92, 97, 102,
    105, 107, 115, 119, 134,
    148
François, Captain (Franchiotto the
    Italian, secret agent), 5
Frankfurt, 53
Frizer, Ingram, 112

Garnet, Henry, 134, 148, 149
Geneva, 49
Genoa, 14
Gerard, Balthazar, 87
Gerard, John, 134, 135, 138, 148
—— Sir Thomas, 40
Germany, 14, 19, 54, 65
Gifford, Gilbert, 92, 93, 94, 98,
    102, 109
—— Dr William, 98, 102
—— George, 106
Gorges, Sir Ferdinando, 126, 128
Gowrie, Earl of, 81
Grant, John, 144, 147
Gregory XIII, Pope, 16, 77, 79, 80,
    82, 83, 88, 90, 96
Gresham, Sir Thomas, 14
Guise, family of, 76, 84
—— Henry, Duke of, 5, 58, 76, 77,
    78, 79, 80, 81, 82, 83, 85,
    86, 95, 109
Gunpowder Plot, 138, 139, 143,
    144, 149, 150

Hall, John, 40
Hamburg, 60
Hamilton, Alexander, 56, 57
—— John, 30
Hampton Court, 137
Harington, John, 126, 144

Harwich, 32, 34, 40
Henri II, King of France, 3
Henri III, King of France, 77, 80, 84
Henri IV, King of France, 114, 115,
    120, 122
Henry VI, King of England, 138
Henry VIII, King of England, 11, 53
Hepburn, James *see* Bothwell, Earl of
Herbert, William *see* Pembroke,
    William Herbert, Earl of
Herle, William, 25, 26, 27, 29
Herries, Lord, 37
Heywood, Jasper, 74
Higford, Robert, 36, 37, 38, 46
Highcliffe, Robert, 106
Hoddesdon, Christopher, 60
Hodgson, Christopher, 98
Holder, Botolphe, 61
Holland, 6, 87
Holt, William, 74, 78, 83
Howard of Effingham, William,
    Lord Admiral, 122, 128
Howard, Henry, Lord, 57, 86
—— Philip *see* Arundel, 13th Earl of
—— Thomas *see* Norfolk, 4th Duke
    of

Ireland, 3, 19, 39, 59, 60, 61, 64,
    78, 123, 124, 125, 129
Isabella, Infanta of Spain, 120
Italy, 54, 111, 119
Ivan the Terrible, 51

Jakhous, Captain, 97
James I and VI, King of England and
    Scotland, 5, 21, 33, 76, 77,
    78, 80, 81, 83, 120, 125,
    127, 129, 130, 131, 132,
    136, 137, 142, 144, 147,
    149
Jenkins, David, 73
Jewel, John, Bishop of Salisbury, 17,
    18
John, Don, of Austria, 58, 59

Keyes, Robert, 140, 141
Kirk O'Field, 7
Kirkcaldy of Grange, William, 37
Knollys, Francis, 94
—— Lettice, Countess of Essex, 113

Knox, John, 49

Lambeth, 139, 140, 141
La Rochelle, 61
Leicester, Robert Dudley, Earl of, 8,
    11, 12, 13, 14, 56, 67, 72,
    91, 108, 113, 116
Lennox, Esmé Stuart, Duke of, 76,
    77, 78, 79, 80, 81
—— Matthew, Earl of, 31, 76
—— Margaret, Countess of, 84
Lepanto, Battle of, 59
Leslie, John, Bishop of Ross, 9, 15,
    21, 22, 23, 25, 26, 27, 28,
    29, 30, 31, 32, 35, 37, 38,
    39, 40
    in the Tower, 41
    makes full confession, 42-3
    goes abroad, 46, 57, 85
Lisbon, 60, 61, 80, 110, 123, 151
London, 5, 14, 19, 21, 23, 29, 34,
    35, 40, 41, 57, 60, 68, 71,
    74, 76, 78, 82, 83, 85, 92,
    96, 98, 101, 106, 110, 111,
    122, 128, 131, 133, 142,
    144, 145, 147, 148, 151
Lopez, Ruy, 116, 117, 118, 119
Lorraine, Charles, Cardinal of, 5
Louvain, 20, 23, 26, 30, 43
Low Countries *see* Netherlands
Lowther, Richard, 7
Loyola, Ignatius, 64
Lumley, John, Lord, 14, 38, 39, 41,
    46
Lyford Grange, 72

Machiavelli, Nicolo, 53
Madrid, 34, 44, 80, 110, 111, 117,
    123
Maitland of Lethington, William, 3,
    7, 8, 9, 21, 37
Mar, John Erskine, 1st Earl of, 81,
    130
Marlow, Christopher, 112
Marshalsea prison, 25, 27, 28, 29,
    68, 69
Mary Stewart, Queen of Scots
    flight into England, 2
    and Treaty of Edinburgh, 3
    and English succession, 4-6

Mary Stewart (*continued*)
enquiry at York and Westminster, 7–9
state prisoner, 10, 11
Norfolk marriage, 12–13, 15, 16, 19, 20, 21, 22, 26, 30, 31, 32, 33, 34, 35, 36, 37, 38, 39, 40, 41, 42, 43, 44
denies knowledge of Ridolfi, 45, 46, 47, 48, 55, 56, 57, 58, 59, 61, 75, 76, 77, 78, 79, 80, 81, 82, 83, 84, 85, 86, 87, 89
transferred to Paulet's custody, 91, 92, 94, 95, 96, 97, 98, 99, 100, 101
trial of, 102–3, 104, 108, 120, 131
Mary Tudor, Queen of England, 18, 53
Maude, Bernard, 97, 98
Mauvissiere, Michel de Castelnau, French ambassador, 83, 84, 94
Mendoza, Bernardino de, Spanish ambassador, 69, 77, 78, 82, 83, 86, 96, 97, 108, 109, 110, 117, 137
Milan, 14
Michelgrove, 74
Mildmay, Walter, 30, 53, 74, 88
Moody, Michael, 108
Moray, James Stewart, Earl of, 5, 8, 9, 12, 45, 51
Morgan, Thomas, 57, 89, 92, 93, 94, 95, 96, 98, 102, 108
Morrison, Dr, 119, 120
Morton, Earl of, 77
Mothe Fénelon, Bernard de Salignac de la, French ambassador, 37
Mounteagle, William Parker, Lord, 136, 139, 143, 145, 146, 147, 149, 150
Mountjoy, 8th Lord *see* Blount, Charles
Munday, Anthony, 105

Naples, 60
Nau, Claude, 99, 102
Netherlands, 2, 6, 10, 19, 22, 23, 30, 31, 34, 35, 47, 49, 54, 58, 60, 62, 68, 77, 81, 82, 95, 105, 113, 121, 140
Neville, Edmund, 88, 89
—— Sir Henry, 20
Newcastle, 106
New Spain, 2
Norfolk, Thomas Howard, 4th Duke of, 7
proposed marriage to Mary Queen of Scots, 8, 11, 12
in the Tower, 13–14, 15, 16
returns home, 20, 21
sends emissary to Spain, 22, 23, 32, 34, 36
re-arrested 37, 38, 39, 40, 41, 42
sentenced to death, 43, 44, 45
executed, 46, 57, 58
Norris, Henry, 1, 5
Northampton, William Parr, Marquis of, 11
Northumberland, Countess of, 23, 26, 28, 30
—— Thomas Percy, 7th Earl of, 12, 13, 17, 19
—— Henry Percy, 8th Earl of, 86
—— Henry Percy, 9th Earl of (the Wizard Earl), 140, 143, 147
Norton, Thomas, 47, 135
Noue, François de la, 59

Oldcorne, Edward, 148
Ousley, Nicholas, 110
Owen, Nicholas, 70
Oxford, 67, 68, 70, 138

Padua, Bishop of, 19
Padua, University of, 53
Paget, Charles, 81, 82, 86, 93, 95, 96, 102, 107, 108
—— Lord, 102, 108
Paris, 1, 5, 36, 46, 49, 50, 52, 60, 61, 65, 77, 78, 79, 95, 96, 105, 107, 108, 110, 117
Parma, Duke of, 81, 87, 95, 98, 110
Parry, Dr William, 88, 89, 90, 91
Parsons, Robert, 67, 68, 69, 70, 71, 74, 78, 79, 80, 81, 84, 95, 105, 107, 120, 133, 134, 138

Paulet, Sir Amyas, 58, 60, 77, 91, 92, 93, 94, 101
Pembroke, William Herbert, Earl of, 11, 13
Percy, Thomas, 140, 141, 142, 144, 147
Percy see Northumberland, Earls of
Perez, Antonio, 116, 118
Phelippes, Thomas, 93, 94, 98, 99, 100, 106, 107
Philip II, King of Spain, 2, 6, 10, 11, 13, 18, 21, 22, 29, 30, 33, 34, 35, 39, 40, 42, 43, 58, 59, 61, 65, 77, 79, 80, 81, 82, 83, 86, 87, 96, 109, 110, 116, 117, 120, 121, 123
Pius V, Pope, 14, 17, 18, 29, 30, 32, 33, 40, 42, 43, 66
Plymouth, 2
Poley, Robert, 98, 100, 112
Portugal, 110, 117
Portugal, King of, 60

Radcliffe, Thomas see Sussex, Thomas Radcliffe, 3rd Earl of
Raleigh, Sir Walter, 121, 127
Rheims, 67, 93, 98, 101, 106, 133
Rich, Penelope, 125
Ridiera, Diego, 1
Ridolfi, Roberto, 7, 11, 13, 14
    interrogated by Walsingham, 15–16
    and Regnans in Excelsis, 17, 19, 21
    leaves England, 22, 23, 25, 26, 28, 29, 30, 31, 32, 33, 34, 35, 36, 38, 39, 40, 42, 43, 44, 45
    dies in Florence, 46, 57, 91
Rogers, Dr Daniel, 59
—— Thomas (aka Nicholas Berden), 77, 97, 106, 107, 109
Rolston, Anthony, 123
—— Francis, 40
—— George, 40
Rome, 19, 29, 32, 34, 44, 51, 54, 59, 60, 66, 67, 68, 70, 71, 77, 80, 89, 92, 105, 106, 131

Rookwood, Ambrose, 144, 147
Rouen, 79, 105, 110, 133
Russia, 51
Rutland, Roger Manners, Earl of, 126

Salder, Ralph, 7, 30, 37, 38, 45
St Bartholomew's Day Massacre, 49, 51, 52
Salisbury, Thomas, 101
Santa Cruz, Marquis de, 111
Santander, 61
Sander, Nicholas, 20, 60
San Lucar, 61
Savage, John, 98, 101, 102
Scotland, 3, 5, 12, 30, 31, 35, 56, 77, 78, 79, 80, 81, 105, 126, 131, 144
Sheffield, Douglas, 108
Shelley, William, 86
Sherwood, Richard, 107
Shrewsbury, Countess of, 9, 20, 58
—— George Talbot, 6th Earl of, 9, 31, 45, 56, 57, 58, 91, 97
Sidney, Henry, 60
—— Philip, 50, 113
Smerwick, 61
Smith, Sir Thomas, 36, 38, 52
Society of Jesus, 64, 65, 66, 134
Southampton, 2
—— Henry Wriothesley, 2nd Earl of, 38, 46
—— Henry Wriothesley, 3rd Earl of, 125, 126, 128, 129
Southwell, Robert, 134, 135
Spain, 1, 6, 11, 15, 22, 33, 34, 35, 40, 49, 54, 60, 95, 110, 111, 117, 119, 124, 131, 137, 139, 142
Spes, don Guerau de, 10, 11, 12, 13, 14, 15, 21, 22, 25, 30, 32, 34, 35, 41, 43, 45
Spinola, Benedict, 14
Stafford, Sir Edward, 108, 109, 110
Standen, Anthony, 111, 116, 118
Stanley, Edward, 40, 41
—— Thomas, 40, 41
—— Sir William, 140
Stewart, Captain James, 77
—— Esmé, Seigneur d'Aubigny see

Stewart, Captain James (*continued*)
Lennox, Duke of
—— Henry *see* Darnley, Henry
Stewart, Lord
—— James *see* Moray, James
Stewart, Earl of
Stockholm, 151
Stonor Park, 71, 74
Stuart, Arbella, 120
—— Charles, 120
Strasbourg, 53
Stukeley, Thomas, 59, 60
Sussex, Thomas Radcliffe, 3rd Earl
of, 30

Tassis, Juan de, 79, 80, 81, 137
Tesimond, Osward (aka Greenway),
148
Throckmorton, Francis, 84, 85, 86,
91, 95
—— Nicholas, 12, 13
—— Thomas, 86
Thurloe, John, 151
Tichborne, Chideock, 101
Tilney, Charles, 101
Tixall, 101
Tower of London, 14, 20, 28, 36,
37, 38, 41, 42, 57, 126, 134,
135, 137
Tresham, Francis, 126, 143, 144,
145, 146, 147
—— Thomas, 136, 143
Tripoli, 54
Tyrone, Earl of, 124

Vega, Antonio de, 117
Venice, 131

Waad, Sir William, 101, 142
Wales, 19
Walsingham, Sir Francis, 5, 6
and Ridolfi, 14–17, 46, 48, 49,
50, 51
early life of, 52–3
and secret service, 54–5, 56, 58,
59, 60, 61, 67, 70, 74, 75,
77, 78, 80
Throckmorton Plot, 83–6, 88
Parry Plot, 89–90, 91, 92, 93, 94
Babington Plot, 96–102, 103,
104, 105, 106, 107, 108
death of, 112, 115, 116, 117,
118, 142, 149, 151
—— Joyce, 53
Ward, Thomas, 145, 146
Warwickshire, 87
Watts, William, 78, 80
Westminster, 8, 9, 137, 141, 144
Westmorland, Charles Neville, 6th
Earl of, 12, 13, 17, 19, 23
Weston, William, 106
William of Orange, 51, 59, 87
Williams, Walter, 105
Wilson, Thomas, 36, 38, 42, 43, 58
Winchester, Amyas Paulet, Marquis
of, 11
Windsor, 74
Windsor, Edward, 97
Winter, family of, 138
—— Robert, 144
—— Thomas, 138, 139, 140, 141,
142, 143, 144, 145, 147
—— Sir William, 61
Wisbech, 107
Wright, Christopher, 141, 142, 147
—— Henry, 144
—— John, 139, 141, 142, 147
Wriothesley, Henry *see*
Southampton, Earls of

York, 7, 140

Zayas, Gabriel de, 22
Zealand, 6, 87
Zutphen, 113